TRAGIC CONSEQUENCES

The Price America Is Paying for Rejecting God and How to Reclaim the Culture for Christ

BY

OLIVER L. NORTH AND DAVID L. GOETSCH

FIDELIS
PUBLISHING

FIDELIS PUBLISHING
ISBN: 9781956454000
ISBN (eBook): 9781956454017

TITLE: Tragic Consequences
SUBTITLE: The Price America Is Paying for Rejecting God and How to Reclaim the Culture for Christ

Cover Design by Diana Lawrence
Interior Design by Xcel Graphic

For information about special discounts for bulk purchases, please contact BulkBooks.com, call 1-888-959-5153 or email—cs@bulkbooks.com

Unless otherwise noted, all biblical quotations are from the English Standard Version. Scripture quoted from the English Standard Version is copyright © 2004 Crossway Bibles, a publishing ministry of Good News Publishers. Used by permission. All rights reserved.

Scripture from Holy Bible, New International Version®, NIV® Copyright © 1973, 1978, 1984, 2011 by Biblica, Inc.® Used by permission. All rights reserved worldwide.

Manufactured in the United States of America

10 9 8 7 6 5 4 3 2 1

Fidelis Publishing, LLC
Sterling, VA • Nashville, TN
fidelispublishing.com

DEDICATION

From Oliver L. North:

For Betsy, with gratitude for her dedication to turning Tragic Consequences in our lives into Blessings.

From David L. Goetsch:

Dedicated with love to my dear family—Deby, Savannah, Ethan, Matthew, and Henry.
I pray God's blessings on each of you.

CONTENTS

PREFACE

Tragic Consequences was written for Americans who are concerned about the cultural decline they see all around them, people who watch the nightly news and ask themselves, "What is happening to our country?" It seems we have become a nation of people who are offended by everything but sin. What is happening to our country is simple to explain but sad to observe: we are seeing what a culture of sin can do to a country. It is a culture of darkness and depravity, a culture lacking in moral restraint, and a culture where life has little value. When a nation rejects God and accepts sin, the lurid stories carried on nightly news programs are the inevitable result.

Because of sin, America's culture has darkened to the point where human life has little or no value, politics resides in the gutter, children are sold into sexual slavery, corruption is rife, mob violence is condoned, pornography is widespread, drug abuse is epidemic, the traditional family is dissolving, and some Americans actually celebrate evil. In spite of this, many churches in America have made sin a taboo subject.

Their pastors tell congregants over and over how God loves them but stringently avoid telling them they are sinners and God hates sin. God hates sin precisely because He loves His children and knows sin will destroy them. We see the tragic consequences of sin every day in this country. If this state of affairs concerns you—as it does many Americans—this book was written for you.

Do you feel helpless in the face of the cultural coarsening infecting American society? Many people do—believers and unbelievers alike. But the good news is you are not helpless—far from it. There is much you can do to encourage repentance on the part of those who reject God and much you can do to help reclaim the culture for Christ. This book offers specific strategies individual Christians and individual churches can employ to turn America from the path of destruction to the path of salvation and freedom.

Tragic Consequences was written with four specific goals in mind. First, to demonstrate conclusively the tragic consequences America is suffering as a nation because leftist politicians, the courts, colleges and universities, the entertainment industry, anti-God organizations, and the mainstream media are collaborating to embrace sin while driving God out of our daily lives. Second, to equip Christians concerned about the cultural darkness surrounding them to shine the light of Christ into that darkness. Third, to challenge churches throughout America to accept the role they must play in reversing the ongoing cultural decline in our country.

The fourth and final goal—a goal encompassing the other three—is to call all Americans, believers and unbelievers alike, to repentance. Achieving this goal is essential. Only by repenting of their rejection of God can unbelievers play a role in overcoming the tragic consequences of sin. Only by repenting of their silence and tepid response to the anti-God crowd can believers play a role in reclaiming the culture for Christ.

Pastor Robert Jeffress described perfectly the role churches must play in reversing the growing cultural decline in America.[1] He said churches have to realize they are not "cruise ships" whose purpose is to make everyone on them comfortable and happy. They are to be more than just safe havens where congregants come to escape the problems of the world. Churches in America must be "battleships" sailing into the midst of a sinful culture, equipping and training their members to do the hard work of reclaiming the culture for Christ.

A CALL TO ACTION AND REPENTANCE FOR ALL AMERICANS

Tragic Consequences does more than document the high cost of sin in America. It also calls on all Americans to repent and take specific steps to reclaim the culture for Christ. This book is a call to repentance for all Americans and a call to action for Christians and churches of all denominations to do their part in replacing sin with righteousness and, in turn, reclaiming the culture for Christ.

As Christians, we are Christ's representatives on earth. Therefore, we can no longer view our churches solely as sanctuaries from the outside world, places of comfort offering us relief from the turmoil we see all around us. Our churches are safe havens, and this is good. They allow us to congregate with like-minded believers who reinforce our beliefs and share our concerns. However, they must also be places of preparation, arming us to go into the world and carry out the Great Commission.

Every day, anti-God ideologues and organizations are scheming to remove any and all vestiges of Christianity from a nation founded on biblical principles and Christian values. Worse yet, they are making steady progress. The more progress they make, the more America's culture—a culture once centered on Christ—is permeated by sin. It is time for Christians to heed the admonishment in Matthew 28:19 to "Go therefore and make disciples of all nations, baptizing them in the name of the Father and of the Son and of the Holy Spirit." This is the most important thing we can do to encourage a nationwide tidal wave of repentance, the first step in reclaiming the culture for Christ.

We have reached a point in our nation's history when Christians must stand and be counted before it is too late. The collapse of our culture is happening because Americans who reject God and accept sin are using the courts and other avenues of attack to drive God out of our lives. Christians cannot justify sitting back and letting this happen. Believers who remain silent about sin and the resultant cultural decline are part of the problem. They are complicit in the decline. Silence in the face of evil is not just ill-advised, it's a sin. This is the message in James 4:17 where we read: "So whoever knows the right thing to do and fails to do it, for him it is sin." If those of us who have given our hearts to Christ won't stand for Him, who will? If those of us who claim to be Christians won't show our neighbors a better way, who will?

Although it is my view Christians should actively engage in politics as part of their civic duty as American citizens, we must understand at the same time that politics will not restore Christ to the center of America's culture. There is only one way to reverse the cultural decline we see all around us; that is for all Americans to repent, give their hearts to Christ, and live according to His Word. This is a message Christians need to share in love with their neighbors who reject God but accept sin. This is a truth *Tragic Consequences* will help you speak in love to unbelievers and believers alike.

OVERALL THEME OF THIS BOOK

The tragic consequences of sin covered in this book are representative of what is happening in America, but the list of problems included herein is not comprehensive. In fact, the cultural and societal problems covered are just the tip of the iceberg. This book describes the kind of problems to be expected in a nation systematically rejecting God and embracing sin.

The theme of *Tragic Consequences* is that the prevailing culture in our country has declined over time because those who reject God and endorse a sinful lifestyle are succeeding in driving Christ out of the everyday lives of Americans. Further, individual Christians and the church have done too little to fight back against these attacks on God and religious freedom for fear of being off-putting or coming under ridicule. Too many churches spend all their time talking about the love of God while ignoring sin. These churches claim they are trying to be "seeker friendly."

Being seeker friendly is a commendable goal, but telling only half the truth about God helps no one. In fact, painting an overly rosy, half-truth version of Christianity inevitably leads seekers to believe they have been misled. People who are lured into church by feel-good platitudes feel betrayed by the church when life after baptism continues to be hard. This is one of the reasons so many young people leave the church. Those testing the water of Christianity need to be told God loves them, but they also need to be told He hates sin. They also need to be told why He hates sin. It's because He loves them. They are His creation, He loves His creation, and He knows sin is destroying His creation.

This book will equip you and your church to speak the truth in love to people whose actions or lack of action are contributing to the cultural darkness we see all around us. The message behind the strategies recommended in *Tragic Consequences* is this: *don't condemn but don't condone.* Rather, share the truth about the inevitable and predicable consequences of sin with those who reject God and point them to Christ as the only way to dispel the cultural darkness engulfing America.

LESSONS FOR TODAY FROM NOAH'S ARK

M ost Christian youngsters learn the story of Noah and his ark at an early age. Many unbelievers who have never opened a Bible are familiar with the story of Noah, at least in general terms. At this point in history when secular humanism is the fastest growing religion in America and sin so dominates the culture, there are important lessons in the biblical story of Noah's ark for Christians and unbelievers. Before examining those lessons, a review of Noah's story is in order.

The fifth chapter of Genesis recounts Adam's descendants down to Noah. Noah first appears in Genesis 5:29 as ninth in descent from Adam. The son of Lamech, Noah is a good man who finds favor in the eyes of the Lord. This is important because, as is described in Genesis 6, the Lord was unhappy with His most important creation: mankind. Sin came to dominate the culture and God hated sin because it was destroying that part of His creation He loved most: His children. Only Noah found favor in the eyes of the Lord. Here is how this situation is recorded in Genesis 6:5–8:

> The LORD saw that the wickedness of man was great in the earth, and that every intention of the thoughts of his heart was only evil continually. And the LORD regretted that he

had made man on the earth, and it grieved him to his heart. So the LORD said, "I will blot out man whom I have created from the face of the land, man and animals and creeping things and birds of the heavens, for I am sorry that I have made them." But Noah found favor in the eyes of the LORD.

God told Noah he was distressed by the wickedness of man and planned, therefore, to destroy all mankind. Only Noah, his family, and seven pairs—male and female—of various kinds of animals would be spared. God commanded Noah to build an ark as a sanctuary for the people and animals he chose to spare. He gave the good man detailed specifications Noah was to follow to the letter. Noah did precisely as he was told by the Lord. Once the ark was built and populated as specified, the Lord sent torrential rain for forty days and forty nights causing a flood to cover the entire earth. The Flood rose higher than the highest mountains. All living things not in the ark perished. The humans and animals on the ark were spared to repopulate the earth.

For those of you reading this having been told the great Flood is a myth, scientific evidence continues to amass to confirm the truth of this story. One of the best books ever written on the subject is *Faith, Form, and Time: What the Bible Teaches and Science Confirms about Creation and the Age of the Universe* by Kurt Wise.

After 150 days, the Flood began to recede, and in the seventh month on the seventeenth day of the month Noah's ark came to rest in the mountains of Ararat. Finally, in the second month of the 601st year on the twenty-seventh day of the month, the occupants of the ark could step out onto dry land (Gen. 8:13–14). Noah built an altar and sent up burnt offerings to the Lord. The Lord was pleased with Noah. He made a covenant with His chosen servant in which He promised to never again send a flood to strike down every living creature on earth (8:21).

There are several especially pertinent lessons for today from this brief recounting of the story of Noah's ark and the great Flood. The first lesson is how displeased God is by the sin He sees in His children. Clearly, God hates sin. If God hates sin, we—His children—must also hate sin and behave accordingly. This is why it is important for churches and individual Christians to tell both sides of the story; God loves humankind and He hates sin and what it does to His creation. This is a message that must be spoken in love continually to unbelievers and believers alike, in church, at work, in the home, and in the public square. What we are observing all around us everyday results from the same thing causing God to be displeased with mankind in the days of Noah: sin.

The second lesson is God is pleased with His children who live righteous lives, just as He was with Noah. This means He expects us to be guided by His Word in everything we think, do, and say rather than by peer pressure applied by sinful people who reject Him. God expects His children to strive for righteousness in their lives and to repent and ask His forgiveness when they fall short. He also expects us to carry out the Great Commission using both words and a consistent Christian example to point unbelievers to Christ. Allowing them to remain comfortable in their ignorance of the gospel is not acceptable to God.

The third lesson is how the judgment of God flooding the whole earth and destroying all humans except the eight He chose, fits into the entire biblical narrative. God created us all to be in community with Him. Our choice for sin instead separates us from Him now and for eternity unless we accept the sacrifice of His Son in payment for our sin. The Flood shows the fate of mankind when we choose to eschew His loving offer. It also shows what happens when there is no God-ordained civil government.

A final lesson from the story of Noah's ark is the world—believers and unbelievers alike—should take no comfort in God's covenant with Noah to never again send a flood to destroy mankind. This covenant does not mean God won't judge mankind as a whole or the individuals who comprise it. He will. Every human being will eventually stand before the seat of judgment. Further, God did not say He won't destroy mankind, just that He won't send another flood to do it.

He might well allow the world to destroy itself, not with a flood of water but with a flood of sin. For example, think of the death and destruction of hell-bent regimes under the likes of Stalin, Mao, and Hitler. God might allow our country to become so infected with sin it is no longer a suitable place to live. In fact, this could be happening right now as we observe the culture being darkened by drugs, alcohol abuse, mass shootings, abortion, mob violence, the dissolution of the family, and other destructive manifestations of sin.

In other words, God might finally give a sinful world that thinks it deserves so much what they really deserve by letting them suffer the consequences of sin, just as individuals experience every day. This is why *Tragic Consequences* is a call to repentance. Only through true repentance on the broadest possible scale can we stop the downward spiral, turn from the path of destruction, and reclaim the culture for Christ.

CHAPTER 1

AMERICA'S BIGGEST PROBLEM

Now the works of the flesh are evident: sexual immorality,
impurity, sensuality, idolatry, sorcery, enmity, strife, jealousy,
fits of anger, rivalries, dissensions, divisions, envy, drunken-
ness, orgies, and things like these. I warn you, as I warned
you before, that those who do such things will not inherit
the kingdom of God.

—Galatians 5:19–21

No nation in the world has been so blessed by God as the United States of America. Our country was founded by men and women seeking something of great importance nonexistent in their native countries: religious freedom. No longer willing to accept the religious persecution perpetrated by the European monarchies of the time, intrepid Christians left their homes and old lives behind, risking everything to establish a new nation on the North American continent. They built that nation on a solid foundation of biblical principles and Christian values. As a result, God blessed the United States richly, making it the most powerful, prosperous, free, and charitable nation on earth. Unfortunately, over time things radically changed.

How would you answer this question: "What is America's biggest problem?" Is it the economy, pandemics, poverty, unemployment, terrorism, competition from China, troubled race relations, nuclear threats from Iran and North Korea, or the national debt? These problems represent important challenges, but not one of them is America's biggest problem. The biggest problem America faces in the twenty-first century can be summarized in one word: sin. As a nation we are systematically rejecting God in favor of a hedonistic, self-serving lifestyle in which individuals view themselves as gods.

Actions have consequences, and the consequences America is suffering for systematically rejecting God are tragic. Sin is dominating America's culture. The culture has declined to the point the kinds of depravity listed in Galatians 5:19–21 are becoming commonplace. A snapshot of contemporary culture in America shows abortion is not just legal but widespread, gun violence is rampant, pornography is ubiquitous, mob violence is a common occurrence, the traditional family has been torn asunder, drug abuse has reached pandemic proportions, and teen suicides are occurring at record levels. Worse yet, these are just a few examples of the tragic consequences being visited upon America as a result of sin.

WHY SO MANY AMERICANS REJECT GOD

It should come as no surprise to Christians that many of their fellow Americans reject God in favor of sin. The depravity of fallen man is described in detail in 2 Timothy 3:1–5:

> But understand this, that in the last days there will come difficult times. For people will be lovers of self, lovers of money, proud, arrogant, abusive, disobedient to their parents, ungrateful, unholy, heartless, unappeasable, slanderous, without self-control, brutal, not loving good, treacherous, reckless, swollen with conceit, lovers of pleasure rather than lovers of God, having the appearance of godliness, but denying its power.

Whether the world is in the last days or not is for God to know, but one thing is certain.

These verses from 2 Timothy are prophetic. They provide a frighteningly accurate description of what is happening in America right now. The rejection of God by mankind is hardly new; it started in the garden of Eden. The fallen nature of man in the form of human depravity coupled with the unrelenting temptations and evil machinations of Satan have always been with us. However, systematic efforts to remove God from all aspects of American life did not gain much traction in America until 1947 when the Supreme Court handed down its politically motivated "wall-of-separation" decision. Then in the 1960s, anti-God activists and organizations gained more ground when the Supreme Court barred sponsored prayer and Bible reading in public schools. Thus began a concerted effort on the part of many Americans to make sin acceptable.

Encouraged by these landmark court cases in the 1940s and 1960s, the efforts of anti-God organizations to remove Christ from the culture have been persistent and unrelenting. The more progress the anti-God crowd makes, the more acceptable sin becomes. The more acceptable sin becomes, the more America's culture declines and, in turn, the more America suffers as a nation. How activists are going about removing God from the everyday lives of Americans is explained in detail in chapter 2 of this book.

THE TRUTH THOSE WHO REJECT GOD NEED TO HEAR

Ironically, many of the people who reject God in favor of sin are concerned about the cultural darkness enveloping them, their communities, and our country. When talking with such people, it is tempting to be ungracious and comment: "What do you expect? This is what life looks like in a nation where sin is accepted but God isn't. If you want to know who is responsible for the cultural decline troubling you, look in a mirror."

While this would be speaking the truth, it would not be speaking the truth in love. Further, this approach would probably cause those who reject God to either become defensive or avoid you altogether. When speaking with people who reject God and accept sin, remember the message in Proverbs 15:1–2: "A soft answer turns away wrath, but a harsh word stirs up anger. The tongue of the wise commends knowledge, but the mouths of fools pour out folly."

As a believer, your goal in speaking the truth to unbelievers about the tragic consequences of rejecting God is to begin a dialogue that eventually leads them to Christ. The truth they need to hear from you is people are not meant to live without God. A nation without God is like a zoo with all the cages left open. People are not designed to set their own parameters and make their own rules. The fallen nature of man renders that approach untenable. Rather, people are designed to live within the boundaries and according to the principles set forth in God's Word.

The cultural decline we see all around us is the result of people doing what Adam and Eve did in the garden of Eden: attempt to establish themselves as equal to God and set their own rules (Genesis 3). There is a name for this approach: sin. It did not work for Adam and Eve, and it is not working for Americans. The only way to reverse the cultural decline infecting all levels of society in this country is for Americans to stop viewing themselves as mini-gods, fall on their knees, and subordinate themselves to the God of Holy Scripture.

As a Christian, you have an important role to play in reversing the downward spiral in America's culture. If you think the job is too big and you are too small, consider this. More than 70 percent of American adults self-identify as Christians; that's more than 210 million believers or, at least, people who claim to be believers. Even allowing for the fact not all people who claim to be Christians actually are, that's still a lot of people. Thus, you are not alone.

Tragic Consequences is a call to arms for you and all Christians who are concerned that America's culture is becoming what is warned of in Galatians 5:19–21 and 2 Timothy 3:1–5. If Christians will come together with the common goal of reclaiming the culture for Christ, we can all be soldiers in a vast army of believers led by God. Further, you are not small. One person armed with prayer and the truth of God is bigger than all of the anti-God activists who are trying to drive Him out of our lives. With Christ on your side, "all things are possible" (Matt. 19:26).

CHAPTER 2

TRAGIC CONSEQUENCES OF REJECTING GOD BUT ACCEPTING SIN

It is better to take refuge in the LORD
than to trust in man.

—Psalm 118:8

The following situations are typical of those reported over and over in the news these days: mob violence broke out in several major American cities, elected officials proposed the legalization of post-birth abortion, gun violence erupted in Chicago killing a child in the crossfire, several teachers were fired for helping students cheat on standardized tests, the teen suicide rate reached an all-time high, and a six-month old baby was shot and killed when an angry driver in a road-rage incident missed his target—the baby's grandmother.

These kinds of incidents have become so common a lot of Americans are wondering, "What is happening to our country?" The answer to this question is simple. As a nation, we have pushed God out of our lives or, in the case of Christians, allowed others to do so. We've darkened the culture to the point human life is no longer valued, drug abuse is rampant, pornography is tearing families apart, and elected officials treat political opponents as enemies to be destroyed.

What is ironic is some of the loudest voices decrying the cultural decline come from the very people whose rejection of God and acceptance of sin are causing it. Many of these people don't even realize the role they play in America's current situation. This lack of awareness is warned of in Proverbs 4:19 where we read: "The way of the wicked is like deep darkness; they do not know over what they stumble."

This lack of awareness on the part of purposefully sinful people who reject God, coupled with their concerns over the increasingly depraved state of the culture, presents Christians with a challenge and an opportunity. The challenge is to stand tall, don the armor of God, and do the hard work necessary to reclaim the culture for Christ. The opportunity is to reach out to fellow Americans who reject God but accept sin and point them to Christ. Only by taking advantage of this opportunity and rising to this challenge will we stop the cultural decline threatening all Americans and restore the culture to Christ.

AMERICA'S CHRISTIAN ROOTS

Historical revisionism is one of the favorite tactics of the anti-God crowd. In revising America's history, they are trying to edit God out of the historical record. Without God setting the standard, it is easy to accept sin. Anti-God activists have been so effective in this regard the majority of Americans, including many Christians, are ignorant of our nation's Christian heritage. For example, many Americans—unbelievers and believers alike—accept the false narrative of activists that our Founders intended there to be a "wall of separation" protecting the people from religion.

These misguided citizens believe God is supposed to be confined to churches on Sunday morning and have no role in government, education, politics, sports, or any other aspect of American life. The truth you can use to set the record straight on this issue is presented in the next section of this chapter, but first a few words about America's Christian heritage are in order.

Anti-God partisans are fond of claiming our Founders were either unbelievers or, at best, deists. Such claims are examples of historical revisionism at its worst. The truth is half of the men who signed the Declaration of Independence held seminary degrees, and the Declaration contains five references to God. The Continental Congress, the governing body of the thirteen original colonies, issued fifteen proclamations over a period of eight years. All fifteen of these proclamations began with pleas to God asking Him to bless the decisions and actions of the Continental Congress. The constitutions of the first thirteen states either required office holders to be Christians or clearly preferred they be.

Does this mean our Founders established America as a theocracy or a nation for Christians only? Absolutely not. In fact, just the opposite is true. Early European settlers came to America in pursuit of religious liberty; they were fleeing religious persecution in Europe. America's earliest settlers wanted to practice the religion of their choice without being coerced by monarchs who made the royal religion mandatory and required citizens to support it through taxation. It was the religious oppression of European kings and queens that drove European colonists to the shores of North America.

In the Europe of those days, religions other than the one prescribed by the king or queen were actively and often brutally suppressed. The Founders were determined this kind of religious coercion would not happen in America, nor did they want a theocracy. Rather, they wanted to ensure the United States was built on a foundation of biblical principles and Christian values. Because of the dedication, courage, and determination of our Founders, this is exactly what happened. America was built on a foundation of principles delineated in the Bible and Christian values drawn from those principles. However, over time, the anti-God crowd undertook a concerted effort to replace that solid foundation with one composed of the ever-shifting sands of secular humanism, a religion in which each individual is his or her own god.

To claim America was built on a foundation of Christian values is not mere conjecture; it's a fact borne out by the historical record. This is why those who reject God find it necessary to revise the historical record. Consider the following excerpt from the Mayflower Compact:

"In the name of God, Amen. We whose names are underwritten . . . having undertaken, for the glory of God, and advancement of the Christian faith . . . a voyage to plant the first colony in the northern parts of Virginia . . ."[1] The intent of America's Founders could not be clearer. Just as an aside, this portion of the Mayflower Compact is now edited out of most public-school textbooks if it is included at all.

Tour our nation's capital and you will find yourself surrounded by evidence of America's Christian heritage. In his book *Rediscovering God in America: Reflections on the Role of Faith in Our Nation's History and Future*, former Speaker of the House of Representatives, Newt Gingrich, provides an excellent summary of this evidence. Let's take a brief tour of the capital courtesy of Speaker Gingrich and see what we find.

In the rotunda of the U.S. Capitol, you will find several historical paintings displayed. Three of these paintings in particular have Christian themes. The first is titled *The Embarkation of the Pilgrims*. This painting depicts a day of fasting and prayer by the Pilgrims. The second painting is titled *Discovery of the Mississippi by DeSoto*. It depicts DeSoto standing next to a monk who prays as a crucifix is placed on the ground. The third painting shows Pocahontas being baptized and is appropriately titled, *Baptism of Pocahontas*.[2]

As you walk through the Capitol, references to faith and God abound. For example, in the Cox Corridor you will find this line from *America the Beautiful* carved into the wall: "America! God shed His grace on thee, and crown thy good with brotherhood, from sea to shining sea." Enter the House Chamber and you will see "In God We Trust" inscribed on the wall above the speaker's podium. Visit the Senate Chamber and you will find the words "Annuit Coeptis" inscribed at the east entrance. The words are Latin for "God has favored our undertaking."

At the southern entrance of the Senate Chamber you will find the words "In God We Trust" inscribed. The chapel for our nation's Capitol contains a stained-glass window showing George Washington in prayer under the words "In God We Trust." The fact the Capitol has a chapel is powerful evidence of a Christian heritage. As an aside, you will find the same words—"In God We Trust"—printed on the cash bills in your wallet or purse. The George Washington window also contains the following words from a prayer: "Preserve me, God, for in Thee I put my trust."[3]

The Washington Monument is a veritable treasure trove of evidence of America's Christian heritage. The capstone originally placed on top of the monument contained the phrase "Laus Deo" which is Latin for "Praise be to God." Other inscriptions within the monument include the following: "Holiness to the Lord," "Search the Scriptures," "The memory of the just is blessed," "May Heaven to this union continue its beneficence," and "In God We Trust" to name just a few. The cornerstone of the monument includes a copy of the Christian Bible.[4]

At the Lincoln Memorial you will find yourself surrounded by the 16th president's words, words reflecting an abiding belief in God. Contained within Lincoln's Gettysburg Address inscribed on the walls of the monument are the words, "We here highly resolve that these dead shall not have died in vain, that this nation, under God, shall have a new birth of freedom." Also inscribed on the wall of the monument is Lincoln's second inaugural address in which he quoted the Bible twice and mentioned God fourteen times.[5]

At the Jefferson Memorial you will find yourself surrounded by references to God made by America's third president. This is ironic because historical revisionists have long held—in spite of copious evidence suggesting otherwise—Jefferson was a deist rather than a Christian. To review, a deist believes God created the world but having done so has no further interest in it. A deist believes God does not concern Himself with the day-to-day lives of people. To them, the earth is like a wound clock left to wind down. The best evidence of the perfidy of historical revisionists in denying the Christianity of Jefferson is found in the great man's own words, many of which are inscribed on his monument.

For example, the interior dome of the monument contains these words from Jefferson: "I have sworn upon the altar of God, eternal hostility against every form of tyranny over the minds of man." A wall panel contains Jefferson's famous words from the Declaration of Independence: "We hold these truths to be self-evident: That all men are created equal, that they are endowed by their Creator with certain unalienable rights, that among these are life, liberty, and the pursuit of happiness."[6]

Jefferson's statements are not the words of a deist, nor do they describe a God who takes no interest in His creation. The treatment of Jefferson by historical revisionists is just one more example of the penchant of anti-God ideologues for deceiving and distorting in order to divide and destroy. What is even sadder than the distortions of historical revisionists concerning Thomas Jefferson is many Christians have allowed themselves to be duped into accepting this false portrayal of our third president. Having heard the lie about Jefferson's faith repeated so often they have come to believe it.

Perhaps the best evidence of Jefferson's Christianity can be found in another wall panel in the monument. In this panel you find these words from Jefferson's *Notes on the State of Virginia* written in 1785: "God who gave us life gave us liberty. Can the liberties of a nation be secure when we have removed a conviction that these liberties are the gift of God? Indeed I tremble for my country when I reflect that God is just, that His justice cannot sleep forever."[7]

If God is just and His justice will not "sleep forever," it stands to reason He is, in fact, interested in His creation. These few quotes only scratch the surface of Jefferson's copious writing, but even a cursory examination of his words belies the claim by historical revisionists that Thomas Jefferson was a deist and America's Founders based their work on anything other than biblical principles and Christian values. When one examines the true and unaltered historical record, it becomes obvious that to deny America's Christian heritage one must be willing to depart from reality and enter the world of fantasy.

During meetings of the Continental Congress, many of the Founders attended services at Christ Church which is located near Independence Hall in Philadelphia. In fact, several signers of the Declaration of Independence are buried at Christ Church. These luminaries of American history are Benjamin Franklin, Benjamin Rush, James Wilson, Francis Hopkinson, Joseph Hewes, and George Ross.[8] One might reasonably ask why these Founders attended Christ Church and are buried there if they weren't Christians.

One of the more vocal of our Founding Fathers was John Adams, second president of the United States. Whereas Thomas Jefferson was a writer, John Adams was a talker. He stated, "The general principles on which the fathers achieved independence were . . . the general principles of Christianity."⁹ America's first Chief Justice of the Supreme Court, John Jay, who was also president of the Continental Congress and coauthor of the *Federalist Papers,* made clear his views on Christianity when he proclaimed, "Providence has given to our people the choice of their rulers; and it is the duty—as well as the privilege and interest— of our Christian nation to select and prefer Christians for their rulers."¹⁰

Anti-God advocates and historical revisionists have worked hard to portray the father of our country, George Washington, as a deist, but again this requires complete ignorance of the historical record. The most famous of George Washington's public speeches is his "Farewell Address." This is the speech in which he announced his intention to step down from the presidency at the end of his second term, an act establishing the two-term precedent now enshrined in law. In this famous speech, Washington said: "Of all the dispositions and habits which lead to political prosperity, religion and morality are indispensable supports. In vain would that man claim the tribute of patriotism, who should labor to subvert these great pillars."¹¹

If God took no interest in the daily affairs of man, religion would not be considered an "indispensable" support. Washington was prescient in knowing there would be people who would attempt to "subvert" the "great pillars" of religion and morality as anti-God adherents are doing with their adherence to secular humanism, agnosticism, and atheism with its acceptance of sin. Unfortunately, those who do not believe in God have no compunction against doing these things, nor do they stop there. Rather than just ignore the historical record, they rewrite it. What is worse, a lot of Americans who are indoctrinated rather than educated naively accept the revised version of America's history.

SEVERING OUR CHRISTIAN ROOTS

How did we go from being a nation established by Christians and built on a foundation of biblical principles to a nation in which God is no longer welcome in the public square? How did we become a nation in which murdering unborn babies is legal, the traditional family structure has been razed, drugs are misused in epidemic proportions, and angry people express their frustration by shooting people in schools, shopping malls, theaters, and retail stores? The answer to these questions is simple. Actions have consequences, and all Americans are suffering the consequences of militant secularists who reject God but accept sin. We are reaping what they have sown.

For more than 150 years, in case after case, the religion clause of the First Amendment was interpreted by the courts as the Founders intended: as a Constitutional protection of religion from government intrusion. Then, in 1947, ignoring legal precedent and acting on their personal beliefs and secular political agenda, the U.S. Supreme Court turned the First Amendment upside down. In one of the most blatant examples of legislating from the bench in the court's history, the justices took a sentence out of context from a letter written by Thomas Jefferson, knowingly misinterpreted Jefferson's words, and used those words to transform freedom OF religion into freedom FROM religion.

A congregation of Baptists in Danbury, Connecticut, became concerned that the government might establish a state religion, an act most likely rendering their denomination not just null and void but illegal. They wrote to President Jefferson seeking his views on the matter. To ease their minds, Jefferson responded with a letter in which he wrote: ". . . I contemplate with sovereign reverence that act of the whole American people (First Amendment) which declared that their legislature should 'make no law respecting an establishment of religion, or prohibiting the free exercise thereof,' thus building a wall of separation between Church & State."[12]

Clearly, Jefferson's letter was intended to relieve the minds of the Danbury Baptists by ensuring them the government would not outlaw or otherwise intrude on their congregation. The "wall of separation" he wrote about was intended to protect the church from the kind of government intrusion associated with European monarchies; the kind the pilgrims came to America to escape. The justices who took Jefferson's sentence out of context, inverted its meaning, and opportunistically misapplied it did so knowingly for the purpose of advancing a secular agenda. Thus began an assault on Christianity that continues to this day.

For decades now, anti-God activists and organizations have been working through the courts and Congress as well as state and local governments to push God out of the lives of American citizens. Ever since secular humanists and atheists appealed successfully to their fellow travelers on the Supreme Court to ban public prayer and Bible reading in the 1960s, elected officials have meekly complied in removing God from the lives of American citizens. The ultimate goal of the anti-God crowd is to outlaw Christianity in America so their sinful way of life can be more easily justified.

In *Engel v. Vitale* (1962) the Supreme Court outlawed sponsored prayer in public schools. Then in *Abington School District v. Schempp* (1963) the high court added insult to injury by outlawing Bible reading and recitation of the Lord's Prayer. Emboldened by these two cases, anti-God activists embarked on a mission to remove God from all aspects of public life in America. Fast-forward to the present and it is obvious they have made substantial and costly progress. The more progress the anti-God crowd makes, the darker America's culture becomes.

Correctly sensing a lack of resolve on the part of public officials and business leaders, anti-God adherents have used lawsuits and the threat of lawsuits to suppress public displays of Christianity in America. They are even attempting to eliminate the term "Merry Christmas" from the American lexicon, preferring to substitute the term "Happy Holidays." Using this generic term allows them to avoid acknowledging who and what Christmas is about. Ardent secularists also encourage the use of "Xmas" instead of Christmas to eliminate "Christ" from the name of the holiday. This ploy makes use of two of their favorite tactics: historical revisionism and semantic subterfuge. Using "Xmas" instead of "Christmas" allows secularists to deny the true origins of the sacred day while also giving it a name that distorts the true meaning of the day (semantic subterfuge).

Not satisfied with removing God from the public square, activists have used threats of negative publicity and boycotts to coerce private businesses into passing anti-Christian policies such as no Bibles allowed on the premises, no framed Bible verses on the walls of offices, and no on-site prayer meetings before work, after work, or during the lunch hour. Although a few stalwart businesses have stood up to the strong-arm tactics of the anti-God crowd, many have meekly caved. Some businesses have gone so far as to make using such terms as "God bless you" or "I will pray for you" taboo.

One of the worst examples of a business caving to pressure from anti-God activists is a company in Florida that refused to allow an employee to park his car on company property because his license plate contained a pro-life message. This action was taken in spite of the fact the plate was authorized and issued by the state and is purchased by thousands of Floridians every year. Anti-God practices such as this, though common, are blatantly unconstitutional. This being the case, why are anti-God activists getting away with these kinds of discriminatory actions?

Activists get away with religious persecution because pursuing a legal remedy forces the believers in question to risk losing their jobs, damaging their careers, and as a result, undermining their ability to provide for their families. They face the ironic situation of winning the battle but losing the war. While we all admire Christian martyrs, few believers want to be one. Consequently, the survival instinct, at least in this case, works in favor of those who reject God but accept sin.

While anti-God supporters have aggressively and unrelentingly pursued their nefarious agenda, Christians have been less assertive in standing up for their Constitutional rights. Opponents of Christianity are winning in part because too many Christians are passively accepting defeat rather than standing their ground. Christians often misinterpret the scriptural message about turning the other cheek (Matt. 5:39) and believe they are proscribed from defending the faith. In this verse, Jesus warns against seeking revenge or retaliating in-kind. He does not proscribe defending Christ, Christianity, or oneself.

Christians also misinterpret the biblical concept of meekness (Matt. 5:5). Meekness is humility, not moral weakness. It does not require Christians to sit back and cede the world to those who reject God. Nor does it mean Christians must allow themselves to be defenseless punching bags for aggressive secularists. Rather, meekness is moral strength equipping believers to be humble. It is an inner strength from knowing you have the Holy Spirit within you and, as a result, Christ working for you. Being meek in the biblical sense means treating the enemies of Christ with Christian love no matter how they treat you, but it does not mean giving into their attacks on God, condoning their actions, or ceding territory to them. Passively giving into those who reject God is weakness not meekness.

Christ was meek but He was not weak. If you doubt this assertion, think of the money changers He threw out of the temple (Matt. 21:12). Further, no matter how harshly He was treated—even in the face of torture and death—Christ stood unflinchingly on God's truth. He spoke the truth in love to those who attacked Him and His father, but Christ never backed down from them or ceded territory to them. Equipping Christians to emulate Christ's example of humble strength is one of the purposes of this book.

Christ used the Parable of the Ten Minas (Luke 19:11–27) to let believers know we are expected to be good stewards of our country and everything else God has blessed us with including our lives, families, property, friendships, and careers. No nation in the world has been more greatly blessed by God than the United States. Consequently, allowing those who reject God to prevail in the current battle for cultural dominance is not good stewardship.

Christians in America must engage because anti-God activists never rest. For example, in 2020 and 2021 they used the COVID-19 pandemic as a convenient excuse to strike another blow against Christianity. Operating on the principle of never letting an emergency go to waste, a number of anti-God governors, mayors, and city council members used claims of public safety as an excuse to shut down churches while allowing bars, liquor stores, and abortion clinics to remain open. As difficult as it is to believe, to some who reject God, seeking solace in a bottle of liquor is an acceptable practice but nourishing the soul through congregational worship is not.

Christians are losing the battle for religious liberty in America. We are losing in the courts, schools, colleges, universities, businesses, and public-square. However, Christians aren't the only losers in this battle. Ironically, those who reject God but accept sin are losing too. All Americans—including those leading the charge against God—are losing. This lose-lose situation is occurring because the tragic consequences of rejecting God affect all Americans, not just Christians.

Metaphorically speaking, all Americans live under the same big roof. When this roof collapses, it crushes everyone under it, not just believers. The cultural roof is collapsing in America and we are all suffering as a result. Christians need to speak this truth in love to their neighbors who reject God but accept sin.

ONLY TWO PATHS FOR AMERICA

Believers and unbelievers who are concerned about the cultural darkness enveloping American society must understand there are only two paths our country can take. One path leads to a culture of hatred, violence, injustice, betrayal, selfishness, frustration, and despair. This is the path America is on now. It's a path paved by the evil schemes of Satan working through his secular minions.

The other path leads to a culture of love, peace, joy, forbearance, kindness, goodness, faithfulness, gentleness, and self-control (Gal. 5:22–23). This is the path paved by the unfathomable love and grace of God. It's the path a nation takes when its guide is Jesus Christ, and its guidebook is the Word of God. There are no other paths a nation can take and there is no middle ground between these paths.

There is no such thing as "religious neutrality," a concept disingenuously promoted by anti-God activists. All people, including atheists, have a god they worship. Christians worship the God of Holy Scripture and are guided by His Word. Atheists, on the other hand, worship the god of self and are, therefore, guided by selfishness. This is one of the reasons the concept of atheism quickly breaks down in actual practice. If human beings are god and, therefore, can determine for themselves what is true and what is right, what happens when one person disagrees with another over what is true or what is right? Predictably, atheism—lacking an unerring source of truth such as the Bible—leads to conflict and chaos.

A nation seeking to supplant God should not be surprised when it is plagued by social problems such as abortion, gun violence, mob violence, human trafficking, child abuse, pornography, cancel culture, drug and alcohol abuse, cheating and lying, road rage, sideline rage, dissolution of the traditional family, gutter politics, teen suicide, and other satanic scourges. These predictable consequences of sin will never be alleviated by politicians or the government. Elected officials and bureaucrats are not strong enough to confront Satan. There is one way and only one way to eliminate the tragic consequences of rejecting God but accepting sin: God's people must repent for having strayed even a micron from the biblical path laid before us and call everyone around us to come along.

For Americans who want to reverse the downward spiral of the prevailing culture, choosing the path of God is the only choice. No other path will lead our country to a place where the cultural darkness currently engulfing us is replaced by the peace, love, and light of Christ. This is a message Christians must speak in love to their unbelieving neighbors. As Christians, we will never enjoy a culture characterized by the fruit of the Spirit until our unbelieving neighbors accept the God of Holy Scripture is the source of that fruit. We must be willing to speak this truth in love to even the most ardent anti-God ideologues. Never forget, silence in the face of evil is the same as condoning evil. When believers remain silent about the sinful behavior they witness, they are complicit in perpetuating that evil.

CHAPTER 3

ABORTION

You shall not murder.

—Exodus 20:13

No consequence of rejecting God but accepting sin can equal abortion in its destructive effects on the culture. Abortion is sin, one of the most tragic consequences America is suffering because of the systematic rejection of God. It is an example of what happens in a culture no longer centered on Christ, a culture left to the worst inclinations of human nature. Abortion not only takes the lives of more than 600,000 babies annually; by so doing it devalues all human life.

It is a very short step from killing babies for the sake of convenience to killing people of any age for equally unjustifiable reasons such as anger, pride, vengeance, and personal gain. This is precisely what is happening in America in the form of mass shootings, mob violence, road rage, and sideline rage. People are killing each other with little or no consideration of right and wrong. Worse yet, the devaluation of human life is a contributing factor in other aspects of America's cultural decline.

When human life has no value, such tragedies as human trafficking and child abuse are no longer abhorrent. Instead, they become normal aspects of the prevailing culture. As a result of the devaluation of human life established by abortion, there are now those among us who view killing another person as an appropriate response when they become angry, frustrated, or just inconvenienced. This is why the nightly news programs are full of gruesome reporting on the latest shootings in big cities and small towns throughout the country.

The case against abortion can be made from the perspectives of science, law, and common sense, but the most important case against it comes from the Bible. Consequently, believers who want to play a positive role in reclaiming the culture for Christ must be prepared to make the biblical case against abortion. Since God's Word is the source of all truth, speaking the truth in love about abortion means speaking from a biblical perspective. Ultimately, all other arguments against abortion—law, science, and common sense—grow out of the biblical case against it.

Christians face a difficult challenge in approaching abortion advocates from a biblical perspective. In rejecting God these advocates also reject His Word, which is the basis of your argument against abortion. It does little good to point out abortion as sin to someone who finds sin acceptable. Consequently, before speaking with an abortion advocate, it is important to understand what you are up against.

Women who undergo an abortion know in their heart they have killed an innocent baby, a heavy burden to carry. Consequently, many women who submit to an abortion find it necessary for their own emotional stability to justify what they have done. This is what has given rise to organizations in celebration of this evil practice. These organizations encourage women to view abortion from the perspective of pride not shame.

The number of women in America who have chosen to have an abortion is now in the millions. For many of them the experience was emotionally traumatic. As you can imagine, this need is deeply felt.[1] The need for justification is at the heart of pro-abortion arguments. It is why abortion advocates cling tenaciously to illogical, outdated arguments lacking in substance. Put simply, they need to be right; the alternative is admitting they murdered an innocent baby.

SEMANTIC SUBTERFUGE IN THE ABORTION DEBATE

Semantic subterfuge is the practice of softening the public's perception of an offensive concept by giving it an inoffensive or even positive-sounding label. With semantic subterfuge, words are used to obfuscate rather than communicate and blur rather than clarify. The point of semantic subterfuge is to make an offensive concept sound more appealing to prevent or, at least, minimize objections to it. Engaging in semantic subterfuge is sin which violates the Ninth Commandment. Verbal and written deception, distortion, and misdirection all amount to the same thing: lying.

Abortion advocates engage in semantic subterfuge when they claim they are "pro-choice" rather than pro-abortion. Calling abortion "choice" is the quintessential example of semantic subterfuge. The term *choice* has a nice ring to it. In the minds of most people, choice is a good thing, a concept with positive connotations. Who doesn't want to have choice in the decisions they make? We like to choose what we eat, who we befriend, what we wear, where we live, what career we pursue, where we vacation, and what hobbies we pursue. Consequently, choice conjures up positive images in the minds of most people.

Abortion, on the other hand, conjures up images of an unborn baby being violently ripped apart in its mother's womb; an image rendering one feeling uneasy at best and overwhelmed with shame at worst. For someone trying to justify an abortion, calling it choice instead of what it really is makes sense. But there is an obvious problem with this strategy. The fact you must find a term other than abortion to describe the procedure means you are ashamed of the procedure. People who can't call something they claim to support what it really is need to take a good hard look in a mirror and ask themselves why.

If abortion were a good thing, there would be no need to engage in semantic subterfuge when referring to it. If it were something to be proud of, people would not be averse to calling it what it is. If abortion weren't an abomination, healthcare professionals who engage in the practice would not feel compelled to dehumanize it by referring to an unborn baby as a "fetus." A biblical truth Christians must be prepared to share with abortion advocates is an unborn baby is just that: a tiny human being. This is the message in Jeremiah 1:5 where we read: "Before I formed you in the womb I knew you, and before you were born I consecrated you . . ."

Believers who want to speak the truth in love to abortion advocates must be prepared to point out the obvious lack of logic in referring to abortion as "choice." If abortion were really about choice, the unborn baby would get a vote. What baby, if it could communicate, would knowingly submit to being killed? What woman who chooses to have an abortion would have wanted her mother to abort her? What child who comes of age would claim he wishes his mother had aborted him? If abortion is really about choice, why do advocates reject the choice not to abort?

Abortion advocates often carry signs bearing the slogan "My Body—My Choice." This is a blatant and obvious false justification. Our earthly bodies are not ours; they are God's. We didn't create our bodies, we didn't earn them, and we did nothing to deserve them. Through the miracle of birth—a miracle of God—we were born with them. This is the message in 1 Corinthians 6:19–20: "Or do you not know your body is a temple of the Holy Spirit within you, whom you have from God? You are not your own, for you were bought with a price. So glorify God in your body."

To make the statement "My Body—My Choice" is to assert a claim that cannot be supported. Further, "My Body" is not the only body involved in an abortion procedure. There is also the baby's body. This is a fact Christians must be prepared to share with abortion advocates when speaking God's truth in love to them.

THE BIBLICAL CASE AGAINST ABORTION

It is important for Christians to be well-versed in the biblical prohibition against abortion because abortion advocates claim there is no such prohibition. They base this argument on the fact the word "abortion" appears nowhere in the Bible. This assertion is an act of desperation, grasping at straws for want of a valid argument. One could make the same argument about child pornography, yet abortion advocates are typically as appalled by child pornography as anyone else.

There are plenty of terms in common usage today that don't appear in the Bible. The Old Testament was written predominantly in Classical Hebrew with some Aramaic mixed in. The New Testament was written in Greek. Consequently, to point out a word which did not even exist 2,000 years ago is missing from the Bible is a pitifully weak argument. New words are added to the English language all the time. Consequently, there are plenty of terms used today by speakers of English that do not appear in the languages of the Bible. However, the messages conveyed by the Bible remain unchanged and are easily discernible to anyone seeking edification rather than trying to justify a weak argument.

The biblical case against abortion is built on two basic premises: 1) Knowingly taking the life of an innocent human being is morally wrong, and 2) Undergoing an abortion is knowingly taking the life of an innocent human being; an unborn baby. It follows logically from these two premises abortion is morally wrong. Therefore, to argue against the first premise is to deny that knowingly killing an innocent human being is wrong.[2] Even for an abortion advocate, this is a difficult argument to support.

To argue against the second premise is to claim one of three possibilities: unborn babies are not human beings, unborn babies are not innocent, or abortion is not intentional. As difficult as it is to believe, abortion advocates have used all three of these arguments to justify their position. This is where the Bible comes into play. Although it does not use the word "abortion," the Bible teaches in the clearest terms killing an innocent human being is wrong.[3]

The two most relevant biblical prohibitions against abortion come from the Sixth Commandment (Exod. 20:13) and the Greatest Commandment (Matt. 22:37–39). The Sixth Commandment is a prohibition against murder. Murdering another human being is abhorrent to God because all human beings are His creation. Not only that, He created all human beings in His own image (Gen. 9:6). Then there is the Greatest Commandment which requires we love our neighbor as ourselves. The Bible is clear that all other human beings—and this includes unborn babies—are our neighbors. Even the most ardent abortion advocate can understand you do not demonstrate love toward your neighbors by killing them.

The Bible forbids the killing of innocent human beings. The term "innocent" is important in the abortion debate. The Bible makes clear, people who are guilty of murder may be required to forfeit their lives (Gen. 9:6). This is because people who are guilty of murder are not considered innocent. Unborn babies on the other hand are the most innocent human beings. They do not yet have the capacity to be anything but innocent. Therefore, it follows logically the Bible forbids the aborting of unborn babies.

The argument used most often by advocates to counter the biblical prohibition against abortion is unborn babies are not human beings. The Bible forbids the killing of innocent human beings. Consequently, if unborn babies are not human beings, they cannot be considered innocent human beings and the biblical prohibition against aborting them is negated. This is a clever ruse on the part of abortion advocates, but that's all it is: a ruse. Even secular scientists acknowledge the first stage of a human being's life occurs at the moment of conception.

A brand-new human life begins the moment a human sperm enters a human ovum. This is the formation of the "zygote," the first human cell. The zygote contains human DNA. The DNA in the zygote contains God's entire plan for the physical development of a human being including such personal traits as hair and eye color. The presence of human DNA at this stage is important because it belies the claim of abortion advocates that an unborn baby is just a "blob of tissue." The zygote stage of life is followed by the "Morula" stage which is, in turn, followed by the "Blastocyst" stage.[4] Like puberty, these stages are all steps in the development of a human being.

Another argument abortion advocates sometimes try to make is a fertilized human egg is not a living entity. Once again science proves the fallacy of this argument. Even at the zygote stage of development, the fertilized egg is an organism meeting all four of the scientific requirements for biological life: metabolism, growth, reaction to stimuli, and reproduction.[5] The fact the zygote is an organism is important because abortion advocates often try to claim it's just a new kind of cell rather than a living organism. Scientists define an organism as a complex structure composed of interdependent elements carrying out the activities of life through separate functions but mutually-dependent organs. The zygote fulfills all aspects of this definition and is, therefore, an organism.[6]

When forced to concede the scientific facts concerning conception, some abortion advocates try to argue the zygote is not a human being because it does not have a soul until after birth. This is a conveniently clever argument because it cannot be proven or disproven, which is precisely why abortion advocates use it. But again, using this argument is an act of desperation undertaken for lack of a valid justification.

As Christians, we know every human being is created in the image of God. Consequently, the moment a human egg is fertilized the resulting human being has a soul. This is not an argument abortion advocates are likely to accept. Consequently, it may be necessary to point out that from a practical point of view their "lacking-a-soul" argument is unacceptable for the very reason they use it: an argument that can be neither proven nor disproven is invalid on its face and, therefore, has no value. Such an argument would not pass muster in a high-school debate.

REFUTING THE CLAIM THAT MOST AMERICANS SUPPORT ABORTION

An argument sometimes advanced by abortion advocates is the majority of Americans support abortion. In their eyes, this makes abortion right. In other words, abortion can be justified on the basis of majority rule. The fallacy of this argument is so obvious one hesitates to point it out. However, Christians who want to speak truth in love to abortion advocates must be prepared to refute even the most inane arguments. Let's apply this same argument to some other issues. Would child pornography be right if a majority of Americans decided it was acceptable? What about sexual slavery? Euthanizing the elderly? Human trafficking? Rape?

One could go on with these kinds of questions, but there is no need. In addition to being an easily-refuted argument, the claim that most Americans support abortion is not accurate in the first place. Support for abortion in America is much weaker than advocates like to claim. Consider the results of the following public opinion polls:[7]

- Sixty-one percent of Americans indicate abortion should be illegal as soon as there is a fetal heartbeat.
- Seventy-two percent of Americans indicate abortion should be illegal after the first three months of pregnancy.
- Eighty-six percent of Americans indicate abortion should be illegal after the first six months of pregnancy.

Christians who want to speak the truth in love to abortion advocates must be prepared to make the point America's Founders were adamant that a democratic form of government had to rest on a foundation of Christian morality or it would soon devolve into mob rule. It wouldn't matter if one-hundred percent of Americans supported abortion, it would still be wrong because what is right or wrong is determined by God not majority rule.

IS INCONVENIENCE SUFFICIENT REASON TO KILL AN UNBORN BABY?

Abortion advocates often argue their case on the basis of exceptions rather than the rule. For example, they often attempt to validate abortion on the basis of the life or health of the mother or the baby. Therefore, it is important for Christians who want to speak the truth in love to their "pro-choice" neighbors to know 92 percent of all abortions performed in America are performed on healthy women who are carrying healthy babies. In other words, 92 percent of abortions are performed in the name of convenience. This statistic comes not from an anti-abortion organization but from the Guttmacher Institute, a pro-abortion organization affiliated with Planned Parenthood.[8]

Arguing on the basis of exceptions is a concept known to debaters as the "exception fallacy." It is akin to concluding all teenagers drive dangerously because you observe one teenager doing so. When speaking the truth in love to an abortion advocate, it is important to argue from the rule, not from exceptions to the rule. To help in this regard, here are the reasons women give most often for choosing to have an abortion:[9]

- The timing is not good—I'm not ready.
- I cannot afford a baby at this time.
- People are depending on me. I already have grown children. I am done with having children.
- My relationship is already troubled; I don't want to wind up a single mother.
- I am too young to be a mother.
- A child would interfere with my education or career plans.

In none of these examples do we see anything about the health of the mother or the baby. In point of fact, all these reasons given for choosing to have an abortion boil down to just one thing: inconvenience. The mothers who cited these reasons were all saying the same thing: having a baby would be inconvenient for them. This being the case, an important question comes to mind you may need to ask abortion advocates: Is inconvenience really a sufficient reason to kill a human being?

WHAT YOU CAN DO ABOUT ABORTION

To play a positive role in preventing abortions, begin by studying what the Bible has to say about this topic. Helpful verses for providing wise counsel to someone who might be contemplating an abortion include the following:

- **Exodus 20:13:** *"You shall not murder."* This verse may help you make the point that calling abortion "choice" does not change the fact it involves killing a living human being created in the image of God, and that doing so is murder.
- **Genesis 1:27:** *"So God created mankind in his own image, in the image of God he created them; male and female he created them."* This verse may help you refute the claim of abortion advocates that an unborn baby is just a blob of inanimate tissue.
- **Job 31:15 (NIV):** *"Did not he who made me in the womb make them? Did not the same one form us both within our mothers?"* This verse may help you make the point to a pregnant woman contemplating an abortion that just as God made her, He also made the baby she is carrying, and that baby has as much right to life as she did.
- **Jeremiah 1:5:** *"Before I formed you in the womb, I knew you . . ."* This verse may help you refute the claim of abortion advocates that an unborn baby is not a human being with a soul.

To speak the truth in love about abortion as part of the wise counsel you provide a pregnant woman contemplating this decision or an advocate of the procedure, you must first know the truth, and God's Word is the truth. Knowing what the Bible says about this issue will equip you to point the way to Christ for pregnant women who may be contemplating an abortion. The verses recommended herein are just to get you started. The Bible has much more to say about the issue of abortion.

Once you have studied what Scripture has to say about abortion, pray God will enter the hearts of pregnant women contemplating the procedure and lead them to make a better decision. Pray for the mother who is struggling and for her unborn baby. Pray also God will use you as His instrument and help you intercede in ways pointing the mother in question to Christ and, in turn, save her baby. If you are not sure how to pray about this issue, approach the Throne of Grace with the following prayer:

> *Lord, (Julie) faces a critical decision. She is contemplating having an abortion. I acknowledge You and You alone can open her eyes, ears, and heart to what Scripture teaches about abortion. I pray You will do so, (Julie's) baby will be spared, and (Julie) will be spared the grief that comes from making an irreversible decision she will regret the rest of her life. Lord, help me help (Julie) in this situation. Give me the words to say and the answers to her questions. Help me approach (Julie) in ways honoring You to show her there are options available other than abortion. It is in the holy name of Jesus I ask for Your intercession in this situation. Amen.*

When you have prayed for the mother and unborn baby you are concerned about, the next step is to make sure your children and grandchildren develop a Christ-centered attitude toward marriage, pregnancy, and children. If we, as Christians, raise our children well, we can reduce abortions substantially in just one generation and maybe even reverse legalization.

Having studied the Bible, prayed, and made sure your children and grandchildren have a biblical image of marriage and children, here are some other things you can do to help reduce the number of abortions occurring in America:

- Put the mother who is contemplating an abortion in touch with mothers who have gone through the process and now regret it. Few people can make a stronger case against abortion than mothers who have submitted to one and now regret their "choice." The *Silent No More Awareness Campaign* is an organization giving women who have had an abortion but now wish they hadn't a forum for expressing their regrets. The *Campaign* began in 2002. Since that time the organization has held more than 2,000 "I Regret My Abortion" events in all fifty states in America as well as seventeen foreign countries. Almost 7,000 women (and men) have shared their testimonies of regret at these events. The *Silent No More Awareness Campaign* can be contacted at the following web address: www.silentnomoreawareness.org.

Referring "pro-choice" mothers to this organization can have a powerful effect on their decision concerning whether or not to have an abortion and whether or not to continue supporting abortion. One of the goals of the *Silent No More Awareness Campaign* is to educate the public and those who might choose to have an abortion about the harmful physical, emotional, and spiritual effects of the procedure.

- Refer women—particularly ardent feminists—who are contemplating an abortion to the organization, *Feminists for Life*. This organization's motto—"Women Deserve Better®"—is a powerful indictment not just of abortion, but of the factors driving women to have abortions. The vision of *Feminists for Life* includes this statement: "A world in which pregnancy, motherhood, and birth-motherhood are accepted and supported."[10] Many feminists are abortion advocates. Consequently, this organization can be particularly helpful when you are trying to speak the truth in love to a woman who is "pro-choice" and also a feminist. *Feminists for Life* may be contacted at the following web address: www.feministsforlife.org.
- One of the most important things you can do to prevent abortions is let pregnant women know they have other options. When speaking the truth in love to women considering an abortion, it is important for Christians to do more than just refute their attempts to justify the unjustifiable. In addition, be prepared to inform pregnant mothers who are considering an abortion about alternatives available to them. This is important because many pregnant women choose abortion out of desperation rather than philosophical acceptance of the concept. Many think they have to have an abortion because it is

the only option available to them. It's not. When it comes to "choice" there are choices other than abortion. There are almost 3,000 pregnancy resource centers (PRCs) in the United States. Some PRCs provide assistance to pregnant women in the form of information and counseling while others provide these kinds of help as well as medical services. PRCs help mothers address the decision about having the child they are carrying and options available to them after the child is born, including adoption. Some PRCs provide baby supplies including formula, diapers, and clothing to mothers who choose to give birth. There are three ways pregnant women can find a PRC near them:[11]

1. Go to www.OptionLine.org (then enter your zip code)
2. Text "Helpline" to 313131
3. Call Option Line at 800-712-4357 (800-712-HELP)

Part of speaking truth in love to "pro-choice" advocates is letting them know abortion is not their only choice.

There is less likelihood desperate mothers will choose abortion when their lives are centered around Christ. Consequently, pointing pregnant women and advocates of abortion to Christ is the most important thing you can do to reduce the number of abortions in America. If you ever find yourself discussing abortion with unbelievers who oppose the procedure or are ambivalent about it, let them know they cannot have it both ways. They cannot continue to reject God and expect there to be no consequences. Abortion is an example of the tragic consequences visited upon a nation that rejects God and accepts sin.

CHAPTER 4

GUN VIOLENCE
AND MASS SHOOTINGS

Do not envy the violent or choose any of their ways.

— Proverbs 3:31 NIV

Next to abortion, few sins demonstrate the tragic consequences of rejecting God more starkly than gun violence and mass shootings. You cannot turn on the nightly news without hearing reports of shootings and not just in large cities but even in small-town America. Gun violence is one more example of what happens to a culture no longer centered on God. It has become all too common for children to be caught in the crossfire of gun battles and be killed by stray bullets. Even churches have been singled out for mass shootings. The prevalence of attacks using firearms has a lot of Americans wringing their hands in fear and frustration. Many Americans wonder what is happening to our country.

When it comes to gun violence, what is happening to our country is this: a lot of Americans reject God but accept sin, and criminal shootings illustrate the point. Those who reject God but accept sin place no value on human life. Because so many Americans are willing to engage in sinful behavior, the culture has declined precipitously. We now have Americans who see nothing wrong with picking up a gun and killing someone to settle a score, act out their frustrations, win a fight, gain attention, or prevail in even a minor dispute. This casual attitude toward human life has caused these assaults in America to reach epidemic proportions.

GUN VIOLENCE IN AMERICA—THE SIZE OF THE PROBLEM

Every day in America more than 300 people are killed or wounded in firearm incidents. The death rate in America from these crimes is close to 40,000 annually. Homicide and suicide account for the majority of these deaths. The focus of this chapter is homicide; suicide is covered in chapter 15. More than 30 percent of gun deaths in America are homicides.[1]

Approximately half of all gun deaths in America occur in large cities. For example, more than 4,000 people are shot or wounded in Chicago every year in gun violence incidents. St. Louis is another hot spot. However, those Americans living in small towns should take no solace from these statistics. In spite of its prevalence in large cities, gun violence is not limited to large cities. For example, Ocala, Florida—a relatively small city—has the highest number of gun-related incidents in America at 28.9 per 10,000 residents.[2]

Because the majority of shootings occur in large cities, one might assume this is an inner-city problem involving drugs and the activities associated with this scourge. This assumption is partially right. Gun violence is an inner-city problem, but not just an inner-city problem. It often involves drugs, but is not just a drug problem. For example, domestic gun violence against women accounts for almost 650 deaths annually, and gun violence is the leading cause of death for teenagers in America. Almost one-million women alive in America today have been shot at or shot by a domestic partner and survived.[3] Although they survived, these women are still victims of gun violence.

One of the reasons Americans are wringing their hands in fear and frustration over the prevalence of gun-violence in our culture is 58 percent of adults in this country or someone they know have experienced it.[4] Even more startling is approximately three million children in

America witness shooting incidents every year.[5] These numbers will just continue to rise until Americans realize this horror is not caused by insufficient gun control measures; nor is it caused by the Second Amendment. Gun violence in America has risen to epidemic proportions because too many Americans reject God but accept sin; they refuse to be guided in their actions by God's Word. People using firearms to wound and kill is a heart problem, not a gun problem.

BLAMING GUNS INSTEAD OF PEOPLE WON'T CHANGE ANYTHING

Because gun violence has become so common in America, it gets a lot of attention from politicians and gun-control activists. Let me state from the outset that shootings will never be curbed by politicians, gun-control legislation, or government policies. This is because gun laws deals with the symptoms of the problem, not the cause—an important point missed or ignored by anti-gun politicians and Second Amendment opponents. This is an important point you might have to make when providing wise counsel to others on the scourge of flying bullets.

Gun violence is not even a gun issue; it is a heart issue. This is a truth that must be spoken in love to those who argue for eliminating or altering the Second Amendment. Gun-control advocates focus on guns when they should focus on the people who misuse them. Trying to curb shootings by eliminating guns is like trying to curb drunkenness by banning alcohol (oh wait, we tried that already). Unless the hearts of people who are willing to use firearms inappropriately are changed, there will continue to be gun violence in America no matter how much gun limiting legislation is passed.

The willingness to kill another individual comes from the heart, not the barrel of a gun. Someone willing to kill to get his way will always find a weapon. Correspondingly, someone who has the love of Christ in his heart will never misuse violence no matter what tools are at his disposal. This is one of the reasons anti-gun activists can't explain away the fact so few legal gun owners ever use their guns against other human beings, and the few who do typically use them in self-defense.

The logic of anti-Second Amendment activists is simple: take away all guns and there will be no more gun violence. On the surface, this assertion appears to make sense, at least in theory. But like so many theories that look good on paper, it breaks down in actual practice. Where this theory goes awry is there is no way to take away all guns. Legal gun owners might comply with confiscatory gun laws, but criminals won't. This is important because it is criminals not legal gun owners who are responsible for the epidemic of shootings in America.

People who use guns inappropriately do so because they reject God but accept sin. They reject the prohibition against murder in the Sixth Commandment. Anyone who will reject God and His Word will also reject laws of all kinds. This is where the supposed logic of gun-control activists breaks down. This is where these activists are shown to be naïve at best and irresponsible at worst. Politicians cannot change the hearts of people who misuse guns, but God can. This is why it is important for Christians to speak the truth in love to misguided haters of firearms.

MASS SHOOTINGS IN AMERICA

Although they account for only a small percentage of the gun deaths in America every year, mass shootings get more attention than the violence occurring every day in larger cities. This is because when a shooting happens in a school, shopping mall, theater, church, or workplace, it hits closer to home for many Americans than reports of gun violence in a big city. People hear reports of the casualties from mass shootings on the nightly news and think, *That could have been me or that could have been one of my children.*

The number of mass shootings in America increases every year. Here are some examples of mass shootings that occurred in various cities across America in just one typical year:

- Six people were wounded when a shooter opened fire at a rodeo/outdoor music venue in Texas.
- Fifteen people were killed or wounded when three men opened fire at a nightclub in South Carolina.
- Ten people were killed or wounded in Mississippi when a shooter walked into a family gathering following a funeral and opened fire.
- Sixteen people were killed or wounded when a shooter opened fire during a backyard party in Rochester, New York.

- Twenty-two people were killed or injured when three men opened fire at a party in Washington, D.C.
- Fifteen people were wounded when a shooter opened fire on mourners leaving a funeral home in Chicago.
- Nine people attending a house party were killed or wounded by a drive-by shooter in Missouri.
- Thirteen people in Louisiana who gathered for a memorial service were wounded when several shooters opened fire.
- Seven people on their way to a party were wounded by a drive-by shooter in Tennessee.
- Eighteen people were killed or wounded in Ohio when a fight broke out between members of opposing motorcycle clubs.
- Six people on a Greyhound bus in California were killed or injured when a passenger on the bus opened fire.
- Seventeen people were killed or injured when a shooter opened fire at a nightclub in Missouri.[6]

The reasons behind mass shootings given most often by secular researchers include the following: 1) a desire for attention and fame, 2) hatred, 3) revenge, 4) ideological issues, and 5) mental health problems. Four out of five of these reasons are heart issues, not gun issues. Yet in spite of this, the debate over how to reduce mass shootings in America focuses on gun-control and, more specifically, on eliminating semi-automatic weapons, especially, "assault rifles."

Changing the hearts of people who are filled with anger, hatred, a desire for revenge, or the need for attention never even comes up. This is why it is important for believers to join the debate over mass shootings and speak the truth in love to those who continually propose strategies having no effect on the problem. People who are serious about reducing the number of attackers using firearms must be willing to address the root cause and stop wasting time proposing feckless measures.

WHAT YOU CAN DO

To play a positive role in reducing gun violence, begin by studying what the Bible has to say about this topic. The Bible makes it clear: violence is an issue of the heart, not the result of owning weapons. Helpful verses for providing wise counsel to people who think the problem can be solved by confiscating guns or eliminating the Second Amendment include the following:

- **Psalm 11:5:** *"The Lord tests the righteous, but his soul hates the wicked and the one who loves violence."* This verse may help you make the point that God not only hates violence, he hates those who engage in it. Therefore, those who engage in violence have a day of judgment coming.
- **Proverbs 3:31:** *"Do not envy a man of violence and do not choose any of his ways . . ."* There is nothing manly, honorable, or admirable about violence. Consequently, people who engage in violence are not to be looked up to or emulated.
- **Titus 3:2:** *"To speak evil of no one, to avoid quarreling, to be gentle, and to show perfect courtesy toward all people."* Acting out one's anger, desire for vengeance, or bitterness toward others in violent ways is wrong. There is a better way to deal with the frustrations of life and it is Christ's way.
- **Jeremiah 22:3:** *"Thus says the LORD: Do justice and righteousness, and deliver from the hand of the oppressor him who has been robbed. And do no wrong or violence to the resident alien, the fatherless, and the widow, nor shed innocent blood in this place."* God expects righteousness from His children, not violence and we are not to engage in violence or other destructive, wrongful acts.

To speak the truth in love about gun violence as part of the wise counsel you provide anti-gun activists as well as people who are not sure where they stand on this issue, you must first know the truth, and God's Word is the truth. Knowing what the Bible says about this issue will help you show those you talk to about gun violence that Christ is the answer to this problem, not additional anti-Second Amendment measures. The verses recommended above show conclusively what God thinks about violence, but they are just to get you started. The Bible has much more to say on this topic.

Once you have studied what Scripture teaches about violence, pray God will enter the hearts of those who place no value on human life and, as a result, are willing to use guns in illegal and destructive ways.

Pray for the perpetrators of gun violence and their victims. If you are not sure how to pray about this issue, recite the following prayer:

> *Lord, we have become a society that places little or no value on the human life You create. I acknowledge only You can change the hearts of people who, because they do not value human life, use guns in illegal and destructive ways. I pray You will enter the hearts of violent people and take away the hatred, anger, fear, frustration, and other factors driving them to misuse guns. Replace these things with the love of Christ and a commitment to honor and obey the Greatest Commandment. I also pray for the victims of these crimes and their families, friends, and loved ones. Help those who believe gun violence can be curtailed by confiscation and repealing the Second Amendment come to realize gun violence is a heart issue, not a gun issue. I ask for Your intercession in this situation in the holy name of Jesus. Amen.*

When you have prayed for God's intercession to stop gun violence, the next step is to make sure your children and grandchildren learn to love their neighbors as themselves, even when they may be angry at them. Children who have the love of Christ in their hearts are not likely to become adults who resort to destructive behavior. If we, as Christians, raise our children well, we can reduce gun violence substantially in just one generation.

Having studied the Bible, prayed, and made sure your own children and grandchildren have learned to love their neighbors as themselves, here are some other things you can do to help reduce gun violence:

- Support community policing.
- Establish outreach programs through your church to mentor boys and young men about the value of human life, particularly those from fatherless households and inner-city neighborhoods where gun violence and crime are common.
- Support organizations trying to reduce shootings such as *Everytown for Gun Safety*. Also teach your children and grandchildren proper firearm safety and usage.

- Encourage your pastor to preach on the sanctity of human life and the scourge of violence.
- Make your church a leader in your community in responding to victims of gun violence with the love of Christ.
- Encourage your pastor to take on the difficult challenge of teaching about the sin of gun violence as well as forgiveness in the aftermath.
- Encourage your church to provide free counseling services for victims and their families.
- Encourage your church to promote reconciliation between perpetrators and victims.
- Encourage your church to establish a jail or prison ministry focusing on rehabilitating people who are serving time for gun violence.

There is less likelihood of criminal shootings in a Christ-centered culture. Be prepared to make this point when speaking the truth in love to people who are concerned about gun violence in our country, including misguided anti-gun activists. Help people realize this kind of violence is a heart issue, not a gun issue, and the solution to it requires focusing on people not guns. Replacing the anger, hatred, bitterness, and frustration filling the hearts of violent people with the love of Jesus Christ is the only way to effectively and permanently curtail gun violence.

CHAPTER 5

MOB VIOLENCE AND DEFUNDING THE POLICE

*Do not plot harm against your neighbor
who lives trustfully near you.*

—Proverbs 3:29 NIV

Mob violence is another of the tragic consequences America is suffering for rejecting God but accepting sin. It is one more example of what happens in a culture no longer centered on Christ. Mob violence is not new in America. There have been riots in our country dating back more than 100 years. In fact, one of the most violent and costly riots in American history occurred in New Orleans in 1866. The backdrop for this riot was the simmering resentment on both sides in the aftermath of the Civil War. It began as a protest against the newly enacted "black codes" but quickly morphed into a riot when protestors and anti-protestors clashed. By the time peace was restored, forty-four people were dead.[1]

The New Orleans riot, like many in America, began as a protest. Not surprisingly, it quickly became violent. This is an important point for Christians who want to speak the truth in love to those who condone or try to justify mob behavior. Riots often begin as peaceful demonstrations. Unfortunately, it takes only a few experienced instigators to transform a demonstration into a riot. Further, the instigators of riots seldom have any interest in the cause of the demonstrators. They use demonstrators as convenient pawns for advancing their own agendas whose purposes typically include looting, arson, anarchy, and violence.

Christians who want to make a positive difference in reducing mob violence can begin by learning the difference between a demonstration and a riot. A demonstration is a form of peaceful protest against perceived inequities. Such demonstrations can take the form of marches, sit-ins, and even boycotts. Peaceful demonstrations are considered a form of free speech and are, therefore, protected by the First Amendment. Peaceful demonstrations were one of the principal strategies of Martin Luther King Jr. and his followers for protesting Jim Crow laws during the Civil Rights Era.

Riots, on the other hand, are not peaceful. They are characterized by violence and destruction and often involve looting, arson, harassment, and bullying. Riots are criminal acts having little or nothing to do with perceived inequities. Therefore, they are not considered a form of free speech protected by the First Amendment. Instigators with shady agendas often transform peaceful demonstrations into violent riots.

THE TRUTH ABOUT MOB VIOLENCE IN AMERICA

Those who reject God but accept sin see nothing wrong with resorting to mob violence to express their perpetual and often manufactured outrage. Evidence of this assertion reemerged in May of 2020 in the aftermath of George Floyd's death at the hands of a police officer in Minneapolis, Minnesota.

Americans of all worldviews and political persuasions found the manner of Floyd's death appalling. Many actually watched it occur on national television and were repulsed by what they saw. As a result, peaceful demonstrations to protest what happened were organized in Minneapolis and several other major American cities, and justifiably so. Unfortunately, as often happens, the peaceful protests did not stay peaceful.

Seeing an opportunity for the kind of destruction and chaos they thrive on, criminal instigators inserted themselves into the peaceful demonstrations. These instigators cared nothing about George Floyd or improving relations between the police and black communities in major cities. Their goal was to bully cities into defunding the police, something criminals find appealing for obvious reasons. The fewer police the easier it is for criminals to do their dirty work.

Unfortunately, weak-kneed public officials in Minneapolis and other large cities went along with the defund-the-police movement. Some went so far as to condone the mob violence, even attempting to justify it as a legitimate form of protest. In the meantime, businesses were looted and shut down, buildings were burned, people were put out of work—including people who supported the peaceful protests on George Floyd's behalf—and innocent bystanders were beaten.

Damage in several major cities ran into the millions of dollars, but the cost in cultural degradation was even greater as copycat riots now spring up nationwide at the drop of a hat. By condoning the riots rather than taking firm steps to shut them down, leftist public officials gave their imprimatur to violence, looting, arson, and anarchy. The destructive mob behavior seen in Minneapolis was repeated in New York, Los Angeles, Miami, Cleveland, Raleigh, Louisville, Atlanta, and Washington, D.C.

It took months for the riots in these major American cities to run their course, but the anarchists who instigated the mob violence weren't done. As the presidential election of 2020 approached, their leaders pre-positioned truckloads of weapons and materials for supporting riots in major American cities. They made no secret of their plans.

If President Donald Trump won re-election, the cities chosen would erupt in violent riots. The unofficial motto of the instigators became "burn it down." These professional rioters and anarchists hate America and use every opportunity to express their hatred in destructive ways. To this day, riots such as those after George Floyd's death have become a common occurrence in major cities across America, particularly those run by leftist-elected officials who condone the violence rather than stopping it.

WHY WOULD PUBLIC OFFICIALS CONDONE MOB VIOLENCE?

As more and more cities across our country have seen peaceful demonstrations purposefully transformed into violent riots, many Americans wonder why some public officials not only refuse to take appropriate steps to curb the violence in their cities but actively condone it. How can elected officials sit back and watch as businesses are looted, public buildings are burned, and lives and livelihoods destroyed?

These are all good questions and the answer to each of them is the same. Those who condone mob violence in America's cities have their own agenda, an agenda that has nothing to do with peace or justice. They have a polar opposite vision for America than that of our Founders' vision. Hence, tearing down America as it now exists is a necessary first step toward achieving their depraved vision, a vision completely devoid of Christ, the Bible, and Christianity.

Public officials who put their secular worldviews and politically correct attitudes ahead of ensuring peace and justice for the citizens who elected them are unworthy of the offices they hold. When they show partiality to the rioters instead of law-abiding citizens, their partiality is a rejection of God. God does not condone partiality. This is the message in Acts 10:34 where Peter says, "Truly I understand that God shows no partiality."

Just and appropriate action on the part of these public officials would have been to protect the innocent, law-abiding citizens whose lives, livelihoods, and businesses were being decimated by anarchists determined to destroy for no reason other than the satisfaction they get from acting out their anger at the world in general.

During the riots in the aftermath of George Floyd's death in 2020, public officials in Minneapolis and other major American cities were willing to condone mob violence to prevent President Donald Trump from appearing strong in the eyes of voters by calling out the National Guard to quell the violence. These public officials were so intent on seeing Donald Trump defeated in his bid for re-election they were willing to sacrifice the lives, businesses, and homes of the citizens they were elected to protect.

Their motives and actions were based primarily on hatred of one individual, a man who in their eyes represented everything they abhor about America. Consequently, they were willing to allow their cities to be ransacked by anarchists if doing so would help bring President Trump down.

It is difficult to comprehend how so much hatred could be directed at one man, but hatred of Donald Trump was a major factor in the riots of 2020. God does not condone human-driven hatred, but the godless do. This is why hate like that demonstrated toward President Trump in 2020 invariably becomes an engrained feature in a culture devoid of Christ. Hate is a predictable feature of a godless culture; it's a fact Christians who want to help curb mob violence must be prepared to tell those who view rioting as an acceptable expression of anger and frustration.

The Bible explains in the clearest terms what God thinks of hatred. In Leviticus 19:17–18 we read: "You shall not hate your brother in your heart, but you shall reason frankly with your neighbor, lest you incur sin against him. You shall not take vengeance or bear a grudge against the sons of your own people, but you shall love your neighbor as yourself. I am the LORD." If public officials in cities torn apart by violent riots will heed this passage from Scripture, they will save lives, livelihoods, and property. They might also save their cities from the downward spiral of abandonment, urban decay, and unemployment brought on by lawlessness as citizens seek safer places to live and conduct business.

DEFUNDING POLICE DEPARTMENTS

The reason our country needs police is too many Americans refuse to be constrained by manners, ethics, laws, or anything else short of force. This is typical of people who reject God but accept sin. If Americans obeyed the Ten Commandments, our country wouldn't need police. Unfortunately, there are a lot of Americans who not only refuse to heed the moral constraints found in God's Word, they refuse to heed *any* constraints. These amoral Americans are easy prey for the professional instigators who incite riots. It requires little to convince people who lack moral restraint to participate in looting, arson, and violence associated with riots.

It should surprise no one that anarchists, instigators, and criminals want to see police departments defunded. The fewer police available to respond to mob violence, the more latitude the inciters have to do their dirty work. With fewer police on the streets, it's not long before those who foment mob violence control the streets. When this happens, as it did in numerous cities in the aftermath of George Floyd's death in 2020, chaos and destruction reign. Let's look at how a number of America's larger cities responded to the absurd defund-the-police demands of violent rioters:[2]

- Austin, Texas cut funding to its police department by $150 million.
- Seattle, Washington cut its police department's budget by $3.5 million.
- New York City slashed theirs by $1 billion.
- Los Angeles, California cut theirs by $150 million.
- San Francisco, California cut $120 million.
- Oakland, California reduced theirs by $14.6 million.
- Washington, D.C. approved a reduction of $15 million.
- Baltimore, Maryland cut $22 million.
- Portland, Oregon cut almost $16 million.
- Philadelphia, Pennsylvania reduced spending on its police department by $33 million.
- Hartford, Connecticut reduced police spending by $1 million.
- Norman, Oklahoma cut $865,000.
- Salt Lake City, Utah eliminated $5.3 million from the budget of its police department.

What happens when police departments are defunded should surprise no one. First, some of the best and most experienced police officers resign or retire while others are laid off. Predictably, the crime rate quickly increases. Both of these things happened as a result of the defund-the-police movement in 2020. In Seattle, the police chief who was a twenty-eight-year veteran of the department and the city's first black police commander, resigned because of the budget cuts. She wasn't alone. In New York City, in just one month, 179 police officers filed for retirement. During the same time period in the preceding year only thirty-five officers filed for retirement.[3]

As a result of the defund-the-police movement, homicides increased by 24 percent in America's fifty largest cities. Gun violence also increased.[4] What is worse is the elected officials who pandered to the mob by reducing police funding in their cities knew crime would increase and law-abiding citizens would suffer as a result. Failure of elected officials to respond quickly and purposefully to mob violence amounts to nonfeasance in office at best and malfeasance at worst. Public officials who are guilty of nonfeasance in the face of mob violence should be removed from office. Those guilty of malfeasance should go to jail.

Elected officials who voted to reduce funding for their police departments may be exempt from being held legally liable for the increased crime and suffering in their cities, but they are not exempt from being held morally liable. If you have occasion to talk with people who support defunding the police, even though they know crime will increase as a result, you might share the message in James 4:17 with them: "So whoever knows the right thing to do and fails to do it, for him it is sin."

Only when all Americans are willing to be guided in their decisions, actions, and behavior by the teachings of Scripture can police departments be defunded. Until that time comes, reducing funding to police departments is folly of the worse kind. Pandering to mob behavior in this way is not just irresponsible, it is unconscionable. This is a truth Christians need to be prepared to speak in love to those who demand cuts to police departments as well as those who try to justify or rationalize mob violence.

WHAT YOU CAN DO

To play a positive role in reducing mob violence in America, begin by studying what the Bible has to say about this topic. Helpful verses for providing wise counsel to people who condone mob violence as well as those who support defunding police departments include the following:

- **Psalm 140:1:** *"Deliver me, O LORD, from evil men; preserve me from violent men . . ."* This verse will help you make the point that violence is evil and the people who perpetrate it or who condone it are also evil.
- **Zephaniah 1:9:** *"On that day I will punish everyone who leaps over the threshold, and those who fill their master's house with violence and fraud."* This verse will help you make the point that those who engage in

mob violence and those who condone it have a day of judgment coming. That day may or may not come on earth but it will come nonetheless.

- **Psalm 73:6:** *"Therefore pride is the necklace; violence covers them like a garment."* This verse will help you make the point that violence grows out of sinister motives. Those who instigate violence as well as those who condone it have a difficult agenda to justify to fair-minded people.
- **Matthew 11:12:** *"From the days of John the Baptist until now the kingdom of heaven has suffered violence, and the violent take it by force."* This verse will help you make the point that violence has always been with us. Therefore, defunding police departments is folly of the worst kind. In a fallen world, there will always be those who refuse to be constrained by any kind of positive motive or beliefs. This being the case, there will always be a need for police.

To speak the truth in love about mob violence as part of the wise counsel you provide to people who might participate in it as well as those who condone it, you must first know the truth, and God's Word is the truth. Knowing what the Bible says about this issue will equip you to point the way to Christ for people who think mob violence is acceptable behavior for the disgruntled, angry, bitter, or frustrated among us. The previous verses are just to get you started. The Bible has much more to say about the issue of mob violence. Once you have studied what Scripture teachers about mob violence, pray God will enter the hearts of people who engage in rioting, looting, arson, and other destructive behaviors as well as those who condone these behaviors. Also pray for the victims of mob violence. If you are not sure how to pray about this issue, recite the following prayer:

> *Lord, I am concerned about the mob violence now so much a part of the culture in America. I pray You will enter the hearts of those who instigate mob violence, those who participate in it, and those who condone this tragic consequence of pushing God out of our lives while accepting sin. Replace the hatred and bitterness of rioters with the love and peace only You can provide so they will*

love their neighbors as themselves. Show those who naively go along with the rioters as well as those who condone mob violence the error of their ways and lead them to Christ so they will come to know a better way. Lord, I ask for Your intercession concerning this issue in the holy name of Jesus. Amen.

When you have prayed for those who engage in mob violence, for those who condone it, and for their victims, the next step is to make sure your children and grandchildren learn how to put the Greatest Commandment into action in their daily lives. Children who learn to love their neighbors as themselves will not grow up to be instigators of mob violence, participants in it, or condoners of it. If we, as Christians, raise our children well, we can reduce mob violence in just one generation.

Having studied the Bible, prayed, and made sure your children and grandchildren know how to put the Greatest Commandment into practice, here are some other things you can do to help curb the mob violence that is perpetrated by people who reject God but accept sin:

- When tragic events cause people in your community to arise, encourage your church and other churches to join together to set an example of demonstrating peacefully. Give angry, frustrated people an alternative to rioting and mob violence.
- Contact public officials and encourage them to adequately fund and properly train police officers and to support them in their efforts to maintain the peace. Do not let the only voices public officials in your community hear be those who demand the police department be defunded.
- Encourage your church and other churches in the community to serve as mediators when tragic events cause people to arise in anger and frustration. There is no better way to work out differences between and among people than using the Word of God.
- In the aftermath of mob violence, provide reconciliation counseling for people who rioted and people who were harmed by the riots. Although the instigators of mob violence are not likely to have any interest in reconciliation, those who let themselves get caught up in

the violence and regret doing so might. Cities torn asunder by mob violence cannot rebuild until there is reconciliation.

• Encourage your church and other churches in the community to be peacemakers by reaching out to people in the community who have grievances, bringing them together with police officers on neutral ground (the church), and promoting dialogue, communication, and relationship building.

There is less chance of peaceful demonstrations morphing into violent riots in a Christ-centered culture. Be prepared to make this point when you speak the truth in love to people who are concerned about the rioting, looting, arson, and violence they see on the nightly news. Help them see mob violence as one more example of what happens in a nation that rejects God but accepts sin.

CHAPTER 6

HUMAN TRAFFICKING

*Rescue the weak and the needy; deliver them
from the hand of the wicked.*

—Psalm 82:4

One of the worst of the tragic consequences of rejecting God but accepting sin is human trafficking. Yet as wicked as this practice is, it is just one more example of what can be expected in a culture devoid of Christ. Human trafficking is the commercial trade of human beings through coercion or fraud. Human traffickers treat their victims as commodities to be illegally traded in the same way they might trade a stolen car or a bag of drugs. Millions of people worldwide—women, children, boys, and men—become victims of human traffickers every year.

Shamefully, the United States ranks high on the list of countries where human trafficking is commonplace. Illegal immigration at America's southern border has increased the volume of human trafficking in this country as evil players prey on unaccompanied women and children. Mexico and the Philippines are also major culprits. Cities in the United States with the most cases of human trafficking every year are Houston, Washington, D.C., New York, Atlanta, Los Angeles, Orlando, Las

Vegas, and Miami. Although human trafficking is largely associated
with larger cities in the U.S., it also occurs in small-towns.[1]

The National Human Trafficking Hotline (1-888-373-7888)
receives almost 150 calls per day from victims of trafficking, concerned
citizens who want to report a suspected case of trafficking, or people
looking for loved ones who might be victims of traffickers. Approximately 17,000 foreign nationals are trafficked into the United States
annually. This fact does not receive the attention it deserves in debates
about the illegal immigration crisis at America's southern border. The
number of American citizens coerced into human trafficking is
unknown but is estimated to be approximately 18,000 annually.[2]

Victims of human trafficking are typically sold as sexual slaves, forced
labor, or human collateral for debt bondage. Debt bondage or debt
slavery involves forcing an individual to work to pay off a debt incurred.
Not surprisingly, those who hold the debt continually add to it so what
is owed becomes perpetual; it's never paid off. Many of the immigrants
who cross America's southern border illegally wind up as debt slaves to
the traffickers who transport them from their native countries.

In some cases, human-trafficking victims are forced to submit to
having their organs extracted. The organs are then sold through a
worldwide black market. The sale of human organs is a huge and thriv-
ing business worldwide. The majority of human-trafficking victims who
are used for forced labor end up working in such industries as commercial sex, hospitality, beauty, agriculture, or construction. Of course,
they have no choice in the matter and are forced to work wherever their
slave masters send them.

As difficult as it may be to believe, human trafficking wasn't even
illegal in the United States until 2000 when Congress finally passed the
Trafficking Victims Protection Act (TVPA). The TVPA established
an office in the State Department to confront the problem. Then in
2008 President George W. Bush signed the William Wilberforce Trafficking Victims Protection Reauthorization Act which reauthorized the
TVPA. The TVPA was reauthorized again in 2013 with added provi-
sions. This reauthorization empowered the Secretary of State to limit
the validity of passports issued to sex offenders to one year and to revoke
the passports of individuals who are convicted of sex crimes.

WHO ARE THE TARGETS OF HUMAN TRAFFICKERS?

Human traffickers target the most vulnerable members of society. They choose their victims primarily from among the homeless, runaways, and unaccompanied illegal immigrants as well as in child foster care, the juvenile justice system, and the child welfare system. Unaccompanied children of foreign-nationals are prime targets for human traffickers because they have no protection. Children are favored targets because they are easier to control, manipulate, and exploit. More than half of all children who become victims of human trafficking came out of the child welfare system.

The typical mode of operation for human traffickers is to exploit the vulnerabilities of their victims by pretending to offer them assistance, friendship, sympathy, jobs, or better lives. This approach is especially effective when used on people who come from abusive homes, who cannot find satisfactory employment, or are addicted to drugs. The following factors put people at high risk of becoming victims of human traffickers:[3]

- Abusive family situations (physical or sexual)
- Drug use
- Homelessness
- Lack of protection from responsible adults
- Poverty (financial distress and seeking a better life)
- Emotional problems (despair, frustration with life, feeling unloved)
- Loneliness (feeling isolated, unable to fit it, rejection)
- Insurmountable debt
- Foster care

Human traffickers quickly size up their victims, identify their points of maximum vulnerability, and exploit those factors. Once an individual becomes a victim of human trafficking, it is difficult to escape the evil clutches of those who engage in this wicked practice. No matter how human-trafficking victims are used—sexual slavery, debt bondage, or forced labor—they come to depend on their slave masters in ways rendering freedom from bondage almost impossible.

SEXUAL SLAVERY AND HUMAN TRAFFICKING

Sexual slavery involves forcing people to engage in sexual activities without their consent. There are several types of sexual slavery associated with human trafficking including commercial sexual exploitation of adults and children, forced prostitution, forced marriage, and cybersex trafficking.

- **Commercial Sexual Exploitation of Adults** involves coercively recruiting, transporting, holding, and/or receiving adults—female or male—for the purposes of sexual exploitation. The United States is a major destination for adults who are being sexually exploited for commercial purposes.[4]
- **Commercial Sexual Exploitation of Children** involves ensnaring, transporting, holding, and sexually exploiting children for commercial purposes. It typically takes the form of child prostitution, child-sex tourism, or child pornography.[5] Child prostitution involves forcing children to serve as prostitutes for the financial benefits of an adult master. Child sex tourism involves buyers traveling to a foreign country for the express purpose of engaging in sex with a child as a commercial transaction financially benefiting an adult master. Child pornography involves using children to make sexually-explicit videos or photographs for commercial purposes. Sadistic child pornography in which the child is tortured is one of the more popular genres for this form of commercial sexual exploitation of children.[6]
- **Forced Prostitution** involves coercing an individual—adult or child—into engaging in sexual activity for the financial benefit of a slave master.
- **Forced Marriage** involves forcing someone to marry without his or her consent. Forced marriage is more common in Asia and Africa than in the United States or Europe.
- **Cybersex Trafficking** involves forcing victims—usually women or children—to perform sexual activities recorded on a webcam while receiving instructions from the paying customer on a split, shared, or separate screen.

Sexual slavery is a form of human bondage where sin-soaked people take control of the lives, limiting or eliminating their autonomy, restricting their freedom of movement, and denying them the right to make their own decisions relating to sexual matters. As difficult as this may be to believe, no matter where you live in the United States, sexual slavery is happening near you.

FORCED LABOR AND HUMAN TRAFFICKING

Forced labor involves using threats, fraud, or violence to coerce people to work against their will. The bulk of forced labor in the United States occurs in domestic work, fishing, agriculture, construction, mining, quarrying, manufacturing, and the sex industry. The need for unskilled labor creates the demand for forced labor. The scourge of poverty ensures a steady supply of forced laborers. Human traffickers provide off-the-books labor for certain industries by luring poor people into their schemes with promises of good jobs and a better life. Estimates of the number of people trapped in forced-labor situations worldwide approach twenty-five million.[7]

The National Human Trafficking Hotline uses a three-part model to distinguish labor trafficking from other forms of labor exploitation: *Action + Means + Purpose.* Labor trafficking occurs when: 1) someone takes specific *action* to engage potential victims by offering them friendship, sympathy, a job, or a better life; 2) the trafficker uses coercion or fraud as the *means* to ensnare victims; and 3) the trafficker's *purpose* is to secure forced labor. The bottom line in defining labor trafficking is the lack of consent on the part of the victim.[8]

ORGANIZATIONS FIGHTING HUMAN TRAFFICKING

Human trafficking is a crime. Consequently, local, state, and federal law enforcement agencies are the first line of defense in combating this heinous practice. In 2001, the FBI established a *Victim's Services Division* employing 300 victim specialists. In addition to law enforcement agencies, there are a number of non-governmental agencies (NGOs) dedicated to stopping human trafficking. These organizations include the following:[9]

- **Truckers Against Trafficking (TAT).** TAT was established in 2009 for the express purpose of putting an end to sex trafficking

within the trucking industry. TAT may be contacted at
www.truckersagainsttrafficking.org.

- **Save Our Adolescents from Prostitution (S.O.A.P.).** S.O.A.P.
provides informative programs during the kinds of large events that
attract sex traffickers (i.e., political conventions and other kinds of
large conferences). S.O.A.P. also distributes millions of bars of soap
with the National Human Trafficking Hotline number printed on
the wrapper to hotels and motels. S.O.A.P. can be contacted at
www.soapproject.org.
- **FAIR Girls.** FAIR Girls is an international anti-trafficking organization providing intervention and care for survivors of commercial
sexual exploitation of children. FAIR Girls can be contacted at
www.fairgirls.org.
- **Karana Rising.** Karana Rising is a non-profit organization based
in Washington, D.C. that helps survivors of human trafficking heal,
pursue education, and find meaningful employment. Karana Rising
may be contacted at www.karanarising.com.

These are just a few of the groups dedicated to fighting human
trafficking. Others include: 8th Day Center for Justice, A21 Cam-
paign, Anti-Slavery International, Arizona League to End Regional
Trafficking, California Against Slavery, Coalition to Abolish Slav-
ery and Trafficking, Girls Educational and Mentoring Services,
Global Centurion Foundation, Hope for Justice, The Samaritan
Women: Institute for Shelter Care, Slavery Footprint, and SOS
International.

All these organizations and numerous others can be located through
an Internet search. Christians who want to help eliminate human trafficking should be familiar with organizations such as these, know the
services they provide, know how to contact them, and be prepared to
make referrals to them.

WHAT YOU CAN DO

To play a positive role in eliminating the scourge of human trafficking,
begin by studying what the Bible has to say about this topic. Helpful

verses for providing wise counsel to victims of human trafficking, their families, friends, and loved ones include:

- **Ezekiel 34:16:** *"I will seek the lost, and I will bring back the strayed, and I will bind up the injured, and I will strengthen the weak, and the fat and the strong I will destroy. I will feed them in justice."* This verse may help you convince family members who are estranged from their lost child they should do everything in their power to rescue her or him from the evil clutches of human traffickers. It may also help you convince your church to get involved in confronting this problem.
- **Isaiah 58:7:** *"Is it not to share your bread with the hungry and bring the homeless into your house; when you see the naked, to cover him, and not to hide yourself from your own flesh?"* This verse may help you recruit other members of your church and the leadership to engage in reaching out to those segments of society most at risk when it comes to human trafficking.
- **Deuteronomy 10:18:** *"He executes justice for the fatherless and the widow, and loves the sojourner, giving him food and clothing."* This verse may help you make the case that intervening with at-risk segments of your community might prevent someone from falling into the evil hands of a human trafficker.
- **Isaiah 1:17:** *"Learn to do right; seek justice. Defend the oppressed. Take up the cause of the fatherless; plead the case of the widow"* (NIV). This verse may help you show others who brush off this problem or choose to ignore it they need to engage and help solve it.

To speak the truth in love about human trafficking to others who may not know it exists or who know someone who has become a victim of it, you must first know the truth—God's Word is the truth. Knowing what the Bible says about this issue will equip you to point the way to Christ for someone who might otherwise be naively lured into becoming a victim of a human trafficker. The verses recommended here are just to get you started. The Bible has much more to say about the issue of human trafficking.

Once you have studied what Scripture teaches about human trafficking, pray God will help you and others provide the kinds of help potential victims need to avoid becoming trapped in this kind of situation. Pray for at-risk individuals and their families. Also pray God will turn human traffickers away from this evil practice and use them to help eliminate it. If you are not sure how to pray about this issue, recite the following prayer:

> *Lord, I am concerned about the abomination of human trafficking and want to help do something about it. I ask that You equip me to play a positive role in eliminating this evil practice, no matter how small and seemingly insignificant that role might be. I also pray You will intercede on behalf of at-risk individuals and help them avoid being lured in by human traffickers while also helping those already ensnared by evildoers escape and rebuild their lives in Christ. Lord, please minister to the families who have lost a child or loved one to this hideous practice and return the victim to them. Finally, I ask You to reach down and touch the perpetrators of human trafficking, turn them from their wicked ways, and show them a better way—the way of Christ. Lord, I ask for Your intercession in this situation in the holy name of Jesus. Amen.*

When you have prayed about this issue, the next step is to make sure you point your children and grandchildren to Christ so they will always have the armor of God to protect them from the scourge of human trafficking. Teach your children to be sensitive to friends who might be walking down a path leading to human trafficking and to speak up to an adult when they see this happening.

Having studied the Bible, prayed, and instructed your children and grandchildren, here are some other things you can do to help eliminate human trafficking:

- Stay informed about this issue and inform others about it. Most people are surprised to learn the scope and depth of this problem.
- Identify at least one organization fighting human trafficking and support it financially.
- Volunteer to work in your free time with an organization in this fight near you.

- Make sure your church's leaders are aware of this problem and encourage your church to support at least one of these organizations.
- Encourage your pastor to bring speakers on this subject into Sunday school classes, Bible studies, youth groups, and prayer breakfasts to inform the congregation about how to recognize the signs of human trafficking and how to identify and assist victims.
- Support political candidates who openly acknowledge the sanctity of human life and are willing to engage on this issue.
- Support legislation and public policies at the local, state, and federal levels aimed at the elimination of human trafficking and treating its victims.

There is no place for human trafficking in a Christ-centered culture. People with Christ in their hearts do not exploit the helpless, defenseless, or downtrodden. Further, God expects His children to speak for those who cannot speak for themselves and to defend those who cannot defend themselves. This means as Christians we cannot justify ignoring the scourge of human trafficking or remaining silent about it.

To do so when we know it exists, possibly in our own communities, is to be complicit in this evil practice. Be prepared to make this point to fellow Christians. There is much work to do to eliminate human trafficking. This work begins by reaching out to at-risk individuals and interceding in ways that prevent them from falling into the hands of human traffickers. If Christians aren't willing to step forward and help eliminate human trafficking, who will?

CHAPTER 7

CHILD ABUSE AND NEGLECT

"Let the little children come to me and do not hinder them,
for the kingdom of heaven belongs to such as these."
—Matthew 19:14 NIV

Christ makes clear in Matthew 19:14 the special place little children hold in His heart. According to Jesus, children belong to "the kingdom of heaven." If children are this important to our Lord and Savior, they should be equally important to us. Consequently, it is difficult to believe anyone would abuse or neglect a defenseless little child. Unfortunately, close to 700,000 children are abused or neglected in the United States every year.[1]

Child abuse is another tragic consequence of a culture devoid of Christ. A culture without Christ at its center is a culture in which Satan rules. In such a culture, child abuse should be expected. Close to 700,000 abused and neglected children every year is hard to imagine, but even worse is the actual numbers are probably higher. Bear in mind these statistics are based on *reported* cases. How many instances of abuse and neglect go unreported? Almost two million children receive abuse-prevention services from child welfare authorities in the U.S. every year.[2]

Scriptural teaching concerning children leaves no doubt about how important children are in the eyes of Christ. Child abuse and neglect are an abomination to the Lord. Psalm 127:3–5 declares: "Behold, children are a heritage from the LORD, the fruit of the womb a reward. . . . Blessed is the man who fills his quiver with them!" This being the case, it's not difficult to imagine what God thinks of those who abuse or neglect them. This is a message Christians must be prepared to speak in love to people who abuse or neglect little children.

CHILD ABUSE AND NEGLECT DEFINED

It is important for Christians to understand what child abuse and neglect are and what they are not. The Federal Child Abuse Prevention and Treatment Act (CAPTA: U.S.C.A. 5106g) as amended by the CAPTA Reauthorization Act of 2010, defines this problem as follows:[3]

- Child abuse/neglect is an act or failure to act on the part of a parent or responsible caretaker that results in the death, serious physical or emotional harm, sexual abuse or exploitation of a child; or
- Any specific act or failure to act that presents an imminent risk of serious harm to a child.

CAPTA defines the term "child" as any person who has not yet reached eighteen years of age or who is not an emancipated minor.[4] An *emancipated minor* is a person under the age of eighteen who has assumed adult responsibilities and is not under the care and control of parents or a guardian. Emancipated minors are responsible for their own care.[5] The most common forms of child abuse are neglect, physical abuse, sexual abuse, and emotional abuse.

CHILD ABUSE AND NEGLECT IN AMERICA

More than 1,500 children die every year from abuse or neglect in the United States. Children one year old or less have the highest rate of abuse and neglect. The most common form of child abuse is neglect; failure to act in the best interests of a child. Neglect puts children in imminent danger of serious physical or emotional harm, sexual abuse, exploitation, and worse yet, it can result in death.[6] A subset of child abuse is sexual abuse, a major problem in the United States. More than

200,000 cases annually of alleged sexual abuse of children are investigated by child advocacy professionals.[7]

More than 75 percent of abused and neglected children are victimized by their own parents. More than 20 percent of child abusers are minors themselves. The most common form of abuse for this group is sexual abuse. Children in families of lower-socioeconomic status are five times more likely to be abused than those from families of higher-socioeconomic status.[8] In addition to neglect and sexual abuse, common forms of child abuse include physical abuse, engaging in violence in front of children, and drug endangerment.

The emotional and psychological damage suffered by the victims of child abuse and neglect can be lifelong. Adult survivors of child abuse are more likely than the general population to experience depression, anxiety, eating disorders, substance abuse, and/or bipolar disorder, often for the rest of their lives. In addition, they are less likely than the general population to finish high school.[9] Subjecting children to violent behavior such as their parents fighting in their presence can also be considered child abuse. Children who are subjected to the violent behavior of adults often suffer the same kinds of emotional and psychological damage as children who are abused or neglected.

DISCIPLINE VERSUS ABUSE

In order to speak the truth in love to people about child abuse, Christians must be able to distinguish between discipline and abuse. The Bible is clear in its expectations concerning discipline. Proverbs 22:6 states: "Train up a child in the way he should go; even when he is old he will not depart from it." Because children—like all human beings—have a fallen nature, disciplining them is part of training them up in the way they should go.

Failing to properly discipline children is itself a form of neglect because it amounts to failing to prepare them for the world they will live in as adults. Proverbs 13:24 states: "Whoever spares the rod hates his son, but he who loves him is diligent to discipline him." This verse suggests applying corporal punishment might need to be part of disciplining a child, a controversial assertion when it comes to the convoluted rules of contemporary childrearing. In some states, spanking a child is considered child abuse and can lead to the intervention of child-protective services personnel.

If corporal punishment is a biblically sound practice, the obvious question is this: How does one distinguish between discipline and abuse? Answering this question requires you to understand the definition of discipline. Discipline as applied to children consists of actions taken to ensure they behave properly and obey the rules. Biblical discipline is distinguished from abuse in why it is applied, how it is applied, and the long-term result it brings.

First, let's consider the "why" of biblical discipline as compared to abuse. Biblical discipline is applied for the purpose of correcting behavior that if ignored might leave the child unprepared to live independently as a responsible member of society. Consequently, biblical discipline is an act of love administered in the child's best interest, an act intended to teach the child a better way. Abuse, on the other hand, is an act of anger, frustration, vengeance, or perversity resulting from either a loss of control or the need to satisfy a perverted desire on the part of the abuser.

Second, let's consider the "how" of biblical discipline as compared to abuse. Biblical discipline is applied in a timely manner—as close to the behavioral infraction as possible. It is also applied in an appropriate way to the infraction in question. Although the Bible certainly accepts properly applied corporal punishment as a form of discipline (Prov. 13:24), this approach is not necessarily appropriate for every infraction.

When discipline is called for, make sure the punishment fits the crime. You don't want to metaphorically prescribe jail time for a parking ticket. Spanking a child for a minor offense may not be the best approach. On the other hand, giving a child a time-out for a major offense is not likely to be effective either. Applying discipline appropriately requires discernment. Never administer discipline to a child in any form when you are in a state of anger or frustration or when your emotions are running high for any reason. Children are not punching bags to be used for releasing pent-up anger. Proper discipline is an act of love—not anger, vengeance, or emotional instability.

To get the best results from discipline, it is important to know your children well enough to understand what forms of discipline work best with them. Children in the same family—even twins—can be quite different when it comes to how they respond to various forms of discipline. For some children, spanking works well; for others it's a waste of time. For some children, isolation for a period of time with no smart phone, computer, television, radio, books, or any other form of amusement works well; for others it doesn't. For some children, just knowing they have disappointed their parents is enough to get them back on the straight and narrow path. With these, a raised eyebrow or a few well-chosen words can be all that is needed.

When it comes to discipline, using the same approach for all of your children is like using the same tool for every repair job. It doesn't work. Sometimes you need a hammer, sometimes a screw driver, and sometimes a wrench. When making repairs to your home, it is important to choose the right tool. The same rule of thumb applies when making repairs to your children's behavior. The *one-size-fits-all* philosophy works about as well for disciplining children as it does for buying clothing for them.

Biblical discipline also involves explaining to the child why he or she is being disciplined and the desired outcome of the discipline. For example, a child who sasses his mother might be given this explanation: "You are going to be disciplined for being disrespectful to your mother. The Bible says children are to honor their mother and father. It is important for you to learn to follow the admonitions set forth in the Bible. When you disobey them, you are disobeying God." Words of correction such as these are similar to the "exhortation" referred to in Hebrews 12:5: "And have you forgotten the exhortation that addresses you as sons? 'My son, do not regard lightly the discipline of the Lord, nor be weary when reproved by him.'"

Children will be better off in life—where they will be subjected to many rules and regulations—if they learn to obey the rules and the admonitions contained in God's Word. Your words of rebuke should make this clear to them. Abuse on the other hand is not about correction, nor is it accompanied by a positive explanation. Rather, abuse is carried out in ways harmful to the child physically, emotionally, and/or sexually. It is not for the child's good. Rather it is the result of the inappropriate impulses of the abuser. Discipline is a positive act that will be appreciated by the child when he or she matures. Abuse is a destructive act that might be resented for a lifetime.

Finally, let's consider the outcome of biblical discipline versus that of abuse. With biblical discipline there may be pain in the short term, but there is gain in the long term. This is the message in Hebrews 12:11 where we read: "For the moment all discipline seems painful rather than pleasant, but later it yields the peaceful fruit of righteousness to those who have been trained by it."

The child who is properly disciplined will be better off in the future for having endured it and, in all likelihood, will realize this at some point down the road. Not so with abuse. With abuse there is pain in the short term and more pain in the long term. The negative effects of abuse can last a lifetime and cause unceasing emotional distress leading to anxiety, depression, PTSD, substance abuse, and other problems.

AT WHAT POINT DOES DISCIPLINE CROSS A LINE AND BECOMES ABUSE?

It is important for Christians who want to speak the truth in love to others about child abuse to understand at what point discipline crosses a line and becomes abuse. Discipline becomes abuse . . .

- when the person administering the discipline loses control of his or her temper and acts out of anger, bitterness, or vengeance rather than love;
- when it is applied to instill fear or establish superiority rather than to edify and correct;
- when it is applied to satisfy some perverse need of the abuser;
- when the child being disciplined is physically injured (e.g., there are bruises, blood, welts, or places where the skin is broken or there is swelling);
- when the person administering the discipline is doing so because the child failed to meet impossible demands or expectations for a child of the age in question to meet;
- when it is inappropriate for the age of the child;
- when it is out of proportion to the infraction.

An important part of a parent's responsibility in raising a child is the appropriate application of discipline. But how does a parent or guardian know if the discipline administered is appropriate? What follows is a brief self-test you can encourage parents and guardians to use to ensure their disciplinary methods don't cross a line and become abuse:

- Does the child understand why he or she is being disciplined?
- Does the child understand what behavior is being corrected and what the proper behavior should have been in the situation in question?
- Does the child understand the discipline is being applied out of love rather than anger, frustration, or perversity?
- Farther down the road when the child has matured, will he or she appreciate the discipline or resent it?
- Would you take the same approach to discipline if another adult were present to observe it?
- When they grow up, is this how you want your children to discipline their children?
- After administering the discipline, do you feel good about it or regretful of your actions?

This self-test will help you speak the truth in love to an adult, parent, or guardian who may be bordering on child abuse in the name of discipline.

RECOGNIZING VICTIMS OF CHILD ABUSE

Child abuse is so common you may know a child who has been abused, although you may not know about the abuse. Adults, parents, and guardians who abuse children become adept at covering the evidence, and children are often afraid to raise the issue or don't know how to go about it. For this reason, it is important you are able to recognize the signs of child abuse. Here are some physical signs that might be evidence of child abuse:

- Bruises, welts, or lacerations that have no explanation or a questionable explanation. Also, bruises, welts, or lacerations in shapes suggesting the use of a whip, belt, or other device
- Bite marks

- Cigarette, rope, or utensil burns
- Broken or fractured bones, particularly on the face
- Broken or missing teeth
- Broken ear drums
- Missing patches of hair (i.e., as if the hair has been pulled out)

In addition to these physical signs of possible child abuse, victims will often display recognizable emotional signs. Emotional evidence of child abuse includes the following:

- Constant crying
- Depression
- Embarrassment over physical injuries and a reluctance to explain what caused the injuries
- Obvious fear of a parent or guardian
- Fear of going home
- Running away
- Fear of physical contact with an adult
- Fear of being left alone with a parent, guardian, or other adult
- Onset of substance abuse

It is important to be careful about jumping to the conclusion a child is being abused. Children often get bumps, bruises, lacerations, broken bones, and other physical injuries as part of growing up. Children can injure themselves even when under the care of the most attentive and loving parents. For example, toddlers just learning to walk are accidents looking for a location. Further, there are reasons other than abuse that children develop emotional problems. However, if you notice a pattern of physical injuries such as those listed herein accompanied by the types of emotional responses listed, there is reason for concern.

WHAT YOU CAN DO

To play a positive role in preventing child abuse, begin by studying what the Bible has to say about this topic. Helpful verses for providing wise counsel to people about child abuse and neglect include the following:

- **Matthew 18:10:** *"See that you do not despise one of the little ones. For I tell you that in heaven their angels always see the face of my Father who is in heaven."* This verse may help you make the point that children hold a special place in the heart of God. If God loves little children, so should their parents, guardians, and siblings. Therefore, to abuse a little child is to risk being subjected to the wrath of God.
- **Luke 17:2:** *"It would be better for him if a millstone were hung around his neck and he were cast into the sea than that he should cause one of these little ones to sin."* This verse may be helpful should you find yourself dealing with an adult who sexually abuses a child or someone who knows of such a person and isn't sure what to do. From this verse, it is clear that God's judgment in such cases is to be feared.
- **Proverbs 22:6:** *"Train up a child in the way he should go; even when he is old he will not depart from it."* This verse may be helpful when you are called upon to provide wise counsel to parents who are concerned about disciplining their children or, worse yet, are afraid to discipline them. This verse will help you make the point that proper discipline is not just essential to the growth and development of children, it is biblical.
- **Matthew 7:12:** *"So whatever you wish that others would do to you, do also to them, for this is the Law and the Prophets."* This verse may be helpful when you are trying to assist parents in distinguishing between discipline and abuse. Commonly referred to as the "Golden Rule," Matthew 7:12 is often stated this way: *Do unto others as you would have them do unto you.* You may want to advise parents who are not sure about how to distinguish between discipline and abuse to apply the Golden Rule in this manner: Don't use any discipline methods with your children you don't want them to use with their children when they grow up or that you wouldn't want used on you.

To speak the truth in love about child abuse and neglect as part of the wise counsel you provide family members, friends, fellow church members, or people in general, you must first know the truth, and God's Word is the truth. Knowing what the Bible says about this issue will equip you to guide people who are struggling with it to Holy Scripture. This is always the best place for them to find the answers they seek. The verses recommended herein are just to get you started. The Bible has much more to say about child abuse and neglect.

Once you have studied what Scripture says about child abuse and neglect, pray God will enter the hearts of those who abuse children and replace the anger, bitterness, frustration, and depravity residing there with the love, patience, and caring of Christ. Also pray God will free children from abusive situations, protect them, and restore them. Pray God will comfort the victims and relieve them of the negative effects of child abuse and neglect. If you are not sure how to pray about this issue, recite the following prayer:

> *Lord, I am concerned about little (Cindy). I know her parents; they are friends of mine, but I fear they might be abusing (Cindy). Lord, help me know what to do in this situation. If it is Your will, use me as Your instrument in making sure little (Cindy) is not or, at least, is no longer abused. Enter the hearts of (Cindy's) parents and take away the negatives that might be causing them to abuse her. Help her parents understand the difference between discipline and abuse. Finally, protect and defend little (Cindy) from abuse and restore her from any abuse that has already occurred. I pray You will wrap this family into Your loving embrace and help them all benefit from the transforming grace of Jesus Christ. I ask for Your intercession on behalf of little (Cindy) and her parents in the holy name of Jesus. Amen.*

After praying for the child you are concerned about and for that child's family, the next step is to make sure you are raising your own children and grandchildren in the instruction and admonition of Christ. Make sure your children and grandchildren are disciplined using measures applied properly, appropriately, and with love. The example you set for them will teach your children and grandchildren what biblical discipline looks like.

Having studied the Bible, prayed, and made sure your children and grandchildren are learning from your example how discipline should be applied, here are some other things you can do to help prevent child abuse:

- Educate yourself about this scourge (learn the information presented in this chapter). Do not take this issue lightly or sweep it under the rug.

- Encourage your pastor to require child abuse prevention training for anyone in your church who supervises children (e.g., nursery workers, Sunday school teachers, deacons, youth pastors, etc.). The number of instances of child abuse in churches would shock you.
- Be prepared to speak the truth in love to neighbors, friends, relatives, and fellow church members about suspected child abuse. To overcome any reluctance you may feel about doing this, remember God expects us to care for and protect the most vulnerable among us. Not only do we have a legal duty to confront this issue, we have a moral and biblical duty.
- Encourage your church to engage on this issue by 1) Providing counseling for victims and perpetrators of child abuse including those who do not attend your church, 2) Making sure your church is a place of healing for victims and perpetrators of child abuse, and 3) Providing open-to-the-public classes for expecting parents and ensure preventing child abuse is part of the curriculum.
- Remember, Christ forgives repentant sinners, even child abusers. Make restoration your goal when dealing with perpetrators of child abuse.
- Make healing and restoration your goal when dealing with victims of child abuse. Let them know God loves them and can give them a new life no matter what they have been forced to endure in the past.

There is less chance of child abuse in a Christ-centered culture. Be prepared to make this point when you talk with others about this critical subject, particularly unbelievers. Help unbelievers understand that rejecting God but accepting sin leads to such tragedies as child abuse and child abuse is one more example of what happens in a godless culture. Let them know a step toward Christ is a step away from child abuse.

CHAPTER 8

PORNOGRAPHY

Put to death, therefore, whatever belongs to your earthly nature, sexual immorality, lust, evil desires, and greed, which is idolatry.

—Colossians 3:5

One of the most tragic consequences of rejecting God but accepting sin is the plague of pornography infecting American society at all levels. Pornography is a silent scourge that has long been with us but has skyrocketed in recent years because of the internet. Internet pornography is an equal-opportunity plague. It is wrecking marriages, careers, and relationships among the rich, poor, and middle-class. The poisonous tentacles of pornography entrap and constrict its victims at home, at work, and even church.

WHAT IS PORNOGRAPHY?

Speaking the truth in love to others about pornography begins with an understanding of what it is. Claiming "I can't define it but know it when I see it" as a Supreme Court justice once did is not sufficient. Therefore, let's begin with a definition of the concept. Pornography is erotic material in any form intended to arouse sexual excitement. Traditionally, pornography was distributed in the form of magazines, books, photographs, and films. But these forms have been surpassed by technological developments.

These days pornography is distributed primarily over the internet—anyone can engage in, produce, and distribute. In fact, the internet has so enabled amateur purveyors of pornography that they are cutting into the profits of pornography professionals. As a result, pornography is more readily available and easily accessible than it has ever been as viewership continues to rise.

PORNOGRAPHY IN AMERICA

Pornography is hardly a new concept in America; it has existed since the earliest years of our nation. By the time our country was founded, Europe—particularly France—was already a major purveyor of pornographic material. Inevitably, this kind of material found its way to America's shores in the baggage of European immigrants. For decades, the pornography industry in America operated on the periphery of society in dark alleys and X-rated shops, but the advent of the internet changed the delivery system in a big way. The internet gave mainstream America instant, anonymous, unfettered access to even the most prurient pornographic material.

Rather than being sold in X-rated shops on the bad side of town, pornography is now readily available to anyone anywhere who has a computer or smart phone. In fact, more than ten percent of all internet sites are pornographic. Consider the following facts about pornography in America:[1]

- Forty million Americans self-identify as internet pornography users. Seventy percent of men aged eighteen to twenty-four visit a pornographic site once a month or more. Men between the ages of thirty-five and forty-nine are the most frequent consumers of internet pornography.
- Of all internet downloads, 35 percent are pornographic. Further, 25 percent of all internet searches are related to sex.
- Pornography use is not limited to men. Approximately 33 percent of all internet pornography consumers are women.

• Ironically, Sunday is the most popular day of the week for viewing pornography.

America has a long history of trying to eliminate pornography or, at least, limit access to it. These attempts have come primarily from governmental bodies such as state legislatures and city councils. Regrettably, though predictably, these efforts have been ineffective. Purveyors of pornography have used the courts to oppose all attempts to curb their trade claiming the protection of the First Amendment.

Opponents of pornography made some headway in limiting it in *Miller v. California* (1973). In this case, the U.S. Supreme Court ruled materials lacking "serious literary, artistic, political, or scientific value" are not protected by the First Amendment's freedom-of-speech clause. Then in 2002, the Supreme Court came close to reversing itself when it ruled in *Ashcroft v. Free Speech Coalition* that pornographic material produced using consenting adults is protected by the First Amendment. This ruling has the effect of protecting those who produce pornography and, by so doing, increasing the amount of pornography produced.[2]

ECONOMICS OF PORNOGRAPHY

Pornography is a multi-billion-dollar business in America. In fact, the industry would generate even more income if not for amateurs cutting into its profits by loading free material on the internet. Hence, pornography is an even bigger plague on American culture than the profit statements of its producers indicate. Annual income generated by Internet pornography alone is estimated to exceed $15 billion.[3]

The income generated by pornography on the internet is substantial but misleadingly underreported. Access to pornography over the internet is much greater than the income figures—as large as they are—might indicate.

LEGAL STATUS OF PORNOGRAPHY

As was stated earlier in this chapter, the Supreme Court ruled in *Miller v. California* (1973) that pornography was not protected by the free-speech clause of the First Amendment. In making this ruling, the Court established what has come to be known as the *Miller Test*. This test established several criteria for determining if written and/or visual material is protected by the First Amendment. The Court ruled material lacking "serious literary, artistic, political, or scientific value" is generally not protected by the First Amendment.

This ruling was a major victory for those opposed to pornography, but it turned out to be a temporary victory. In 2002 the Supreme Court handed down a ruling in *Ashcroft v. Free Speech Coalition* that affords First Amendment protection to pornographic material produced using only consenting adults.[4] With this ruling, pornography—except child pornography—became legal in the United States. However, there is an exception. It is illegal to import material considered "obscene" or "immoral." The U.S. Customs and Border Protection agency interdicts pornographic material imported into the United States on the basis of the Smoot-Hawley Tariff Act of 1930.[5]

CHILD PORNOGRAPHY IN AMERICA

Child pornography is a particularly vile and destructive form of child abuse that has exploded in recent years because of the internet. In 2004 the National Center for Missing & Exploited Children maintained 450,000 files on child pornography victims. By 2019 that number grew to seventy million files and has been growing since.[6] Child pornography is one of the more popular forms of this evil concept.

Child pornography is defined in Section 2256 of Title 18, United States Code as ". . . any visual depiction of sexually explicit conduct involving a minor (someone under eighteen years of age). Visual depictions include photographs, videos, digital or computer-generated images indistinguishable from an actual minor, and images created, adapted, or modified, but appear to depict an identifiable, actual minor."[7]

This definition also encompasses undeveloped videotapes and any electronically stored data that can be converted into visual images meeting the definition of child pornography. Further, in the case of child pornography, federal law supersedes state and local definitions of the age of consent. When it comes to child pornography, the age of eighteen applies no matter how an individual state might otherwise define the age of consent.[8]

Penalties for violating federal law pertaining to child pornography are severe. A first-time offender convicted of producing child pornography can be sentenced to fifteen to twenty years in prison. A first-time offender convicted of transporting child pornography can be sentenced to five to twenty years in prison. Penalties may be increased to life imprisonment if the following circumstances exist:[9]

- The pornographic images are violent, masochistic, or sadistic
- The minor in the pornographic images was sexually abused
- The person producing the pornographic images has prior convictions for sexually exploiting children

WHO ARE THE MOST COMMON CHILD-PORNOGRAPHY OFFENDERS?

Some of the most common offenders in the production of child pornography are the parents or guardians of the children victimized. Friends or neighbors known to the children targeted are also common exploiters. These offenders are all people who have ready access to the children targeted and are trusted by those children. The actual statistics are shocking: 18 percent of child pornography images are produced by the victim's parent or guardian and 25 percent by a neighbor or family friend. On-line exploiters who entice children into going along with the production of pornographic images account for another 18 percent.[10]

Sextortion is a growing component of the child-pornography industry. Sextortion as it applies to child pornography means threatening to reveal sensitive secrets about the victims or to harm them or their loved ones if they don't submit to being used in the production of pornographic material.[11] Sextortion is one of the reasons for the rise in the number of cases of self-assisted child pornography. Self-assisted child pornography is the production of pornographic images in which the child cooperates in the production of the material, often following instructions provided online by an exploiter.

WHAT YOU CAN DO

To play a positive role in eliminating pornography from the culture, begin by studying what the Bible has to say on this topic. Helpful verses for providing wise counsel to people who have been ensnared by pornography or family members or friends who are concerned about them include the following:

- **Matthew 5:28:** *"But I say to you that everyone who looks at a woman with lustful intent has already committed adultery with her in his heart."* This verse may be helpful if you have occasion to speak the truth in love about pornography to someone who thinks just watching pornography is acceptable, particularly married men and women who are ensnared by this wicked phenomenon.
- **1 Corinthians 6:18–20:** *"Flee from sexual immorality. Every other sin a person commits is outside the body, but the sexually immoral person sins against his own body. Or do you not know that your body is a temple of the Holy Spirit within you, whom you have from God? You are not your own, for you were bought with a price. So glorify God in your body."* These verses may be helpful if you have occasion to provide wise counsel to fellow Christians who are letting themselves be seduced by pornography. They know or, at least should know, their bodies are temples for the Holy Spirit. Therefore, you can remind them how defiling themselves with pornography is defiling the temple of God.
- **1 Corinthians 10:13:** *"No temptation has overtaken you that is not common to man. God is faithful, and he will not let you be tempted beyond your ability, but with the temptation he will also provide the way of escape, that you may be able to endure it."* This verse may be helpful if you have occasion to speak the truth in love to someone who claims he cannot help himself because the temptation of pornography is too much for him. This verse will help you make the point the individual in question is no different than anyone else. We are all tempted, but those of us who turn to God for help are bolstered by His strength and given a way to escape the temptation of pornography.

- **1 John 2:16:** *"For all that is in the world—the desires of the flesh and the desires of the eyes and pride in possessions—is not from the Father but is from the world."* This verse may be helpful when you have occasion to talk with someone who claims pornography is harmless. This verse makes the point that pornography comes not from God, but from Satan. Therefore, it is harmful by definition since everything about the devil is harmful.

To speak the truth in love about pornography as part of the wise counsel you provide for brothers and sisters in Christ as well as unbelievers, you must first know the truth, and God's Word is the truth. Knowing what the Bible says about this issue will help you point the way to Christ for people who are being drawn by the seductive lure of pornography. The verses recommended herein are just to get you started. The Bible has much more to say about the issue of pornography.

Once you have studied what Scripture teaches about pornography, pray God will enter the hearts of people caught up in this wickedness and take away the lust ensnaring them. Also pray for people who produce pornography, both professionals and amateurs. Finally, pray for the worst victims of this scourge: young children who are forced to participate in the production of pornography by adults they trust. If you are not sure how to pray about this issue, recite the following prayer:

> *Lord, I am concerned pornography is wreaking havoc on marriages, families, the church, and society in general. I ask You to touch the hearts of those who produce pornography and turn them from their wicked ways and strengthen those who are taken in by this addiction. Help them resist the temptation of pornography. I pray most fervently for Your protection of children from pornography and restore those who are forced by adults they trust to participate in the production of pornographic materials. Finally, Lord, I ask You to help me play a positive role—no matter how small—in helping fight this darkness. I ask for your intercession in this situation in the holy name of Jesus. Amen.*

When you have prayed for the victims as well as those who produce pornography, the next step is to make sure your children and grandchildren learn what the Bible teaches about sexual purity. If we, as Christians, raise our children right, we can reduce the scourge of pornography substantially in just one generation.

Having studied the Bible, prayed, and taught your own children and grandchildren about God's expectations concerning sexual purity, here are some other things you can do to help eliminate pornography from the culture:

- Equip yourself with the information in this chapter so you can speak the truth in love to others on this critical subject.
- Get your church involved in combating pornography. Encourage your pastor and other church officials to talk about the issue rather than ignoring it. Don't let pornography become the elephant in the living room everyone avoids.
- Encourage your church to provide recovery and restoration counseling for pornography victims and offenders.
- Be Christlike in dealing with pornography addicts. Make your goal their restoration, not condemnation or punishment (see 1 Cor. 6:9–11 for guidance).
- Encourage your church to provide strong Christian mentors for people who give in to the temptation of pornography.
- Take advantage of the materials, information, and assistance available from anti-pornography organizations and agencies such as the Family Research Council (www.frc.org).
- Encourage your church to provide classes on how parents, guardians, and other adults can interdict internet child pornography. Such classes should cover at least the following strategies: 1) Developing an online safety plan before allowing children access to the internet, 2) Supervising children who use the internet, 3) Adjusting privacy settings on computers and using parental-control technologies, 4) Teaching children they should never share personal information or images over the internet, 5) Teaching children about body safety and appropriate boundaries, 6) Being alert to signs of sexual abuse (e.g., attempts on the part of children to conceal their online activities, unexplained changes in behavior, anxiety, depression, and

angry outbursts), 7) Teaching children to tell a parent, guardian, or another adult if they are approached for sexual favors online, and 8) Reporting suspected enticement or exploitation attempts immediately by calling 911 or contacting the FBI at www.fbi.gov/tips.[12]

Pornography might not go away in a Christ-centered culture, but it will be much less of a problem. But in a culture devoid of Christ, pornography will thrive just as it is doing now. Be prepared to make this point when you speak the truth in love to believers and unbelievers on this subject. The fastest and most effective way to drive pornography out of the culture is to put Christ back in the culture. Pornography is one more example of what happens in a nation that rejects God but accept sin.

CHAPTER 9

CANCEL CULTURE AND CENSORSHIP

"These things I command you, so that
you will love each other."

—John 15:17

Imagine being vilified, persecuted, and fired from your job for simply stating an opinion someone didn't like. Imagine being afraid to state an opinion for fear of being ostracized, defamed, disparaged, or worse. If you find these things hard to believe, don't. Though straight out of Orwell, these things are happening in America right now. In fact, they have become commonplace. The concept is known as the *cancel culture*, and George Orwell predicted it in his landmark book, *1984*. Orwell's only error was in being off a few years in the date.

The cancel culture is one more tragic consequence of rejecting God but accepting sin. It is a predictable consequence of pushing Christ out of the culture. Like so many of the problems currently affecting American society, the cancel culture has been magnified by social media. The internet has emboldened and empowered those who use social media to destroy the lives of people whose opinions don't conform to leftist orthodoxy. However, the weapons used by cancel culture advocates are not limited to just character assassination on social media or the politics of personal destruction. For cancel culture practitioners, any and all methods—including censorship—to suppress opposing views are on the table.

CANCEL CULTURE DEFINED

The cancel culture is an outgrowth of political correctness. To review, political correctness is a form of speech and thought control in which certain terms, phrases, and opinions are deemed taboo by those who dominate the prevailing culture. Not surprisingly, when those in positions of dominance are anti-Christian ideologues, biblical truth is deemed politically incorrect as are terms, phrases, and opinions associated with traditional American values. In fact, terms and phrases deemed politically incorrect by those against Christianity, including many directly from the Bible, are often labeled "hate speech" and subjected to censorship.

Labeling words or opinions they disagree with as hate speech is a favorite tactic of those who promulgate the cancel culture. How ironic to hear the words of Jesus labeled as hate speech when in Matthew 22:39 He commanded us to love our neighbors as ourselves. But then, the irony is lost on those who reject God, accept sin, and make it their goal to push Christ out of the culture. To those against God, even contradictions this obvious fail to register.

Political correctness is enforced by "canceling" people who express opinions or use terms or phrases the anti-Christian activists dominating the culture do not agree with or do not like. It is an approach to controlling speech and discouraging dissenting opinions in which people who say or write anything deemed politically incorrect are ostracized or censored. The concept is the polar opposite of free speech. In fact, the unstated motto of cancel-culture practitioners is, *agree with us or we will destroy you.* The ultimate goal of cancel-culture practitioners is to frighten opponents into self-censorship, to make them so afraid to speak out they choose to remain silent for fear of repercussions.

The free-speech clause of the First Amendment was enacted for the sole purpose of protecting speech, writing, and other forms of expression some people might consider controversial, objectionable, or even offensive. After all, offensive expression is the only kind needing protection. The primary methods of cancel-culture advocates are social media attacks against individuals, censorship, and threats of boycotts or bad publicity against businesses and other organizations and institutions. Unfortunately, these nefarious methods are working. More than half of Americans are afraid to speak their minds for fear of being canceled, and this includes pastors and priests. Further, fear of bad publicity and boycotts has turned many business leaders into corporate cowards who pander to anti-God and leftist thinkers—supporting their causes and making financial donations to their organizations—in hopes of protecting themselves and their businesses from cancel-culture attacks.

In a Christ-centered culture, people with differing opinions can disagree without being disagreeable. Christ did not tell us to love our neighbors only when they agree with us. Further, people with Christ in their hearts do not try to ruin each other over differing opinions, nor do they viciously attack those who disagree with them. Believers are warned against using cancel-culture tactics in James 4:11 where we read, "Do not speak evil against one another, brothers." Remove Christ from the culture and it becomes a cancel culture, a culture in which people not only speak evil against those they disagree with, they try to destroy them.

In a Christ-centered culture, people discuss and debate differing opinions, but with the cancel culture those who disagree must be destroyed. In a Christ-centered culture, people are afforded the right to hold differing opinions and even make statements some might find offensive. In a cancel culture, differing opinions and statements deemed politically incorrect are cause for vicious attacks and concerted efforts to ruin the offender's life, even if the offender's statements are true. In a Christ-centered culture, God's Word is the truth. In a cancel culture, truth isn't even a consideration. Those who hold opinions at odds with today's culture must either keep their opinions to themselves or suffer the wrath of cancellers.

What makes the cancel culture especially dangerous is one undeniable fact: anything anyone says is going to offend someone. America is a diverse, pluralistic nation made up of people from varied backgrounds who espouse differing worldviews, political opinions, religious tenets, and personal beliefs. This being the case, one can hardly utter a word without offending someone. Further, in the culture currently prevailing in America being offended is the new national pastime. More people play the *I-am-offended* game than play football, baseball, basketball, and soccer combined. It seems in the America of today, people are offended by everything but sin.

It is especially important you be informed about the cancel culture because Christians are most often victims of it. Christians have been attacked by cancel-culture practitioners for saying something as positive and well-intended as "God bless you." In fact, words normally a part of the Christian's vocabulary have been branded "hate speech" by those who reject God but accept sin.

American citizens have been attacked by cancel-culture advocates for supporting the "wrong" political candidate. Actors and actresses have been cancelled for taking a political stand out of step with the Hollywood elite. College professors have been canceled for teaching the truth about American history. What the cancel culture ultimately cancels is free speech, free thought, and free expression.

FREEDOM OF SPEECH VERSUS THE CANCEL CULTURE

One of the cornerstones of our constitutional republic is freedom of speech. It is a bedrock right granted by God and enshrined in the Bill of Rights of the U.S. Constitution which reads as follows:

> Congress shall make no law respecting an establishment of religion, or prohibiting the free exercise thereof, or **abridging the right of freedom of speech,** or of the press, or of the people to peaceably assemble, and to petition the Government for a redress of grievances.[1]

Many Americans have been erroneously taught freedom of speech is a right granted by the government. In truth, freedom of speech is a gift from God acknowledged by the government. The Founders merely incorporated this and other God-given rights into the Constitution when they wrote the Bill of Rights to delineate what the federal government was charged with protecting. To speak the truth in love to people about the cancel culture and to show them a better way, Christians must be well-versed concerning the First Amendment and God's gift of freedom of speech. Here are some facts about freedom of speech all Christians should know:[2]

- The Supreme Court interprets freedom of speech broadly to encompass talking, writing, printing, using the internet, and various forms of expression such as displaying flags, wearing armbands, and even burning flags.
- Although the First Amendment prohibits "Congress" from inhibiting free speech, the Supreme Court interprets it more broadly to include all government agencies and officials at the federal, state, and local levels. The First Amendment is intended to protect individuals from government.
- The First Amendment does not protect individuals from the machinations of private organizations. With only limited exceptions, private businesses are allowed to inhibit free speech. This is how the big-tech giants controlling social media are getting away with censoring and de-platforming Christians and conservatives.
- The Supreme Court has ruled there can be restrictions on certain types of speech with "low" First Amendment value. These low-value forms of speech include defamation, threats, obscenity, child pornography, and commercial advertising.

RIGHTS VERSUS RESPONSIBILITIES

One of the truths you may have to speak in love to practitioners of the cancel culture is this: with every right comes a corresponding responsibility. In other words, just because someone has the right to say offensive or hurtful things does not mean they should. Words are powerful; they can uplift or tear down, build up or destroy, calm or incite. Because of this, believers and unbelievers alike should choose their words carefully and consider the effect their words might have on others.

With this point made, a caveat is in order. No one is suggesting Christians or anyone else should be *politically correct*. On the contrary, Christians should always speak the truth, but with due consideration of the listener's feelings. Political correctness, on the other hand, is an enemy of truth. Political correctness is a favored tool of cancel-culture practitioners. In actual practice the concept is about politics not correctness. It is used as a way to control speech, discourage dissent, and promote an agenda. The role political correctness plays in the cancel culture is explained later in this chapter. The concept Christians should adopt is known as *tact*.

When interacting with people, particularly those whose views differ from yours, being tactful is important. Tact encourages dialogue while ill-considered or angry words encourage conflict. This is an important message for believers and unbelievers. Think of tact as driving in the nail without breaking the board or making your point without making an enemy. Assume you are having a conversation and you disagree with something the other individual said. Here are two ways you might express your disagreement: 1) "That is the dumbest idea I've ever heard," or 2) "I hear what you are saying but you might want to think that idea through more carefully."

Both responses indicate disagreement, but the former is hurtful while the latter is tactful. Which response would you prefer if you were the recipient? The first response would probably shut down further communication or worse. It might even incite conflict. But the second response would encourage continued dialogue. Tact is an outgrowth of the Greatest Commandment. Choosing to be tactful rather than hurtful when we disagree is an act of love toward a neighbor.

When speaking the truth in love to cancel-culture practitioners or anyone else, an important point to make is this: you will never convince anyone of your opinion by attacking, defaming, or otherwise alienating them. You don't win converts to your cause, no matter what that cause may be, by attacking those you disagree with. This is an especially important truth for Christians to heed because our overriding goal is always to steer unbelievers to Christ. Tact will help you achieve that goal. It is an important part of speaking the truth in love to others.

SEMANTIC SUBTERFUGE AND THE CANCEL CULTURE

A favorite strategy of cancel-culture practitioners is *semantic subterfuge*. This ploy is the polar opposite of speaking the truth in love. The concept involves polishing the images of offensive and even heinous concepts by renaming them using soft-sounding, appealing terms.

Semantic subterfuge is about deceiving rather than edifying, obfuscating rather than communicating, and distorting rather than clarifying.

Perhaps the best example of semantic subterfuge is referring to abortion as *choice*. Abortion is the true and factual label for the process of killing an unborn baby in its mother's womb. But the term conjures up disturbing images in the minds of people, as it should. To overcome this inconvenient fact, abortion advocates disingenuously adopted an inoffensive term for this offensive practice, a term meant to relieve advocates of the disturbing images raised by the truth.

They selected the term *choice* and, by doing so, transformed the subject of the debate from infanticide to a woman's right to choose. Which is why abortionists often refer to this crime as *women's health*. Unlike abortion, choice conjures up positive images in the minds of people and, therefore, generates less opposition. Who doesn't want to have choices when it comes to making life's decisions? Of course, what goes unsaid by abortion advocates is the choice they are so enamored with is the choice to kill an innocent baby.

Other examples of semantic subterfuge include referring to rioters as demonstrators, looters as protestors, lying as misspeaking, legalized discrimination against biological women in favor of transgenderism as equality. The fastest way to get in hot water with the anti-God crowd these days is to use terms other than those deemed politically correct by the cancel-culture police. Consequently, a truth you may have to speak in love to cancel-culture practitioners is this: when you have to call a concept something other than what it really is, you need to look in a mirror and ask yourself why.

POLITICAL CORRECTNESS AND THE CANCEL CULTURE

Cancel-culture advocates define *political correctness* as choosing words carefully to avoid offending others or hurting their feelings. If this were an accurate description of political correctness, the concept would be less controversial, but it's not. As has already been clarified, choosing your words carefully to minimize offense or harm is tact, not political correctness. Tact has nothing to do with politics, while political correctness has everything to do with it, and not just politics, but the politics of anti-God activists and leftist thinkers.

Political correctness is yet another example of semantic subterfuge. As practiced in today's culture it's not about correctness or even tact. Rather, it is a form of speech and thought control. The concept is used to suppress free speech and free thought without having to admit to doing so. This is important for Christians to understand because speaking the truth in love to unbelievers is likely to be deemed politically incorrect and almost certain to put you at odds with cancel-culture practitioners. This, then, raises an interesting question: What constitutes politically correct speech?

This is a difficult question to sort out because the answer is subjective and always changing. On the other hand, it is easy to describe what kinds of speech are likely to be deemed politically incorrect. Any words, phrases, or statements cancel-culture advocates disagree with will be labeled politically incorrect or, worse yet, hate speech. For example, the Bible uses the term "man" to encompass all of humankind. Read in context, it is obvious the term includes men and women. However, use the term "man" to describe humankind in today's culture and you will suffer the self-righteous, manufactured indignation of the political-correctness police.

When it comes to political correctness, the goal of cancel-culture zealots is to control or at least influence what words and labels are acceptable in daily discourse. The concept is applied for the purpose of forcing people to adopt, accept, and use certain terms that have entered the lexicon by means of semantic subterfuge. Hence, it is deemed politically incorrect, for example, to refer to a woman's choice to terminate a pregnancy as abortion. On the other hand, using such pejoratives as "Bible thumpers" and "Jesus freaks" to describe Christians is deemed acceptable. This anomaly reveals one of the least admirable aspects of political correctness; it is based on a double standard.

Understanding the concept of political correctness is important for Christians because biblical truths—those you want to speak in love to others—are often deemed politically incorrect in a culture devoid of Christ. Consequently, Christians should be prepared to become targets of the cancel culture for speaking God's truth. If this happens to you, speak God's truth anyway. It is always better to please God than to please those who reject Him but accept sin.

God's truth is a stubborn concept. No matter how much people try to avoid it, suppress it, or distort it, God's truth eventually rises to the surface and demonstrates its validity. Further, when you are armed with the truth of God you have nothing to fear from the cancel culture or the political-correctness police. One courageous Christian fortified by the armor of God is more than a match for even the most ardent anti-God activists and organizations.

INTERNET "FLAMING" AND THE CANCEL CULTURE

Flaming is a concept birthed on the internet. It means posting highly insulting, profane, and even hostile messages on the internet about another person or that individual's postings. Hiding behind the shroud of online anonymity, flamers express their disagreement in angry, insulting, demeaning, and even destructive terms. An individual who flames another online would probably be too inhibited to do so in person, but the anonymity of the internet can embolden even the most timid among us. Flaming allows irresponsible people to engage in unacceptable behavior without fear of consequences.

Flaming is a written form of verbal aggression. Hence, it can be used to bully people into retracting dissenting opinions or refusing to state opinions in the first place for fear of online retribution. This is the intimidation aspect of flaming. The unstated message flamers trying to intimidate others send is this: "State an opinion different than mine and you are going to be attacked." Because people who are not well grounded in God's Word are susceptible to criticism from their peers, flaming is an effective way to suppress dissenting opinions and discourage inconvenient questions. This is why it is a favorite tactic of cancel-culture advocates.

It is important for Christians to be aware of the odious practice of internet flaming and to be undeterred by it. This is because speaking God's truth online is a sure way to attract the attention and wrath of flamers. In fact, when you are flamed for posting the truth of God, it just means you are being an effective representative of Christ. Those who reject God are never comfortable hearing His truth. When you walk with God, you step on Satan's toes. The harder you step, the louder he screams. When Christians are flamed by unbelievers, it is really Satan acting out his frustration through the writing of his minions.

If you are flamed by someone who is offended by God's truth, before responding—if you respond at all—think of what is written in Proverbs 15:1–4: "A soft answer turns away wrath, but a harsh word stirs up anger. The tongue of the wise commends knowledge, but the mouths of fools pour out folly. The eyes of the LORD are in every place, keeping watch on the evil and the good. A gentle tongue is a tree of life, but perverseness in it breaks the spirit." Your soft answer might turn away the flaming wrath of an unbeliever and show that individual a better way.

Accustomed to people responding in-kind to their insults, profanity, and diatribes, flamers might be influenced in a positive way by a different kind of response. However, even if they aren't, resist the natural human urge to respond the same negative way to a flamer. As a Christian, you realize no one is anonymous on the internet or anywhere else. God is watching and He sees all, hears all, and knows all. This is the message in Psalm 139:4 where we read, "Even before a word is on my tongue, behold, O LORD, you know it altogether." God knows how you respond, so make sure your responses honor Him while also pointing flamers to Christ.

SOCIAL MEDIA CENSORSHIP

Another tool of cancel-culture advocates is censorship on social media. One of the fastest ways to cancel an individual or organization in the age of electronic communication is to deny them access to social media. The practice is known as de-platforming. It is important for you to understand the issue of censorship because Christians who use social media for speaking God's truth may find themselves censored and de-platformed.

Censorship involves suppressing the free exchange of information, speech, or communication—including electronic communication—by claiming the material being censored is objectionable, harmful, or likely to incite destructive behavior. It is important for Christians to understand the First Amendment protects them from being censored by the government—with a few specific exceptions—but not by private enterprises. Private enterprises such as the big tech companies that own the largest social media platforms are legally empowered to censor material loaded on their platforms, at least for now.

The controversy over social media censorship arose when it became clear big tech companies were censoring material for political reasons rather than for the good of the public. The criticism made against social media giants is they censor only material that doesn't comport with the political views of the owners. For example, many political conservatives have been denied access to social media by big tech companies whose political views differ from theirs. Perhaps the best-known example of this phenomenon occurred when Twitter took down then-President Donald Trump's account and refused him access from that point forward.

To be clear on this issue, for now private companies have the legal right to censor the material posted on their sites. However, this does not excuse them from legitimate criticism. Having a legal right to censor material does not give these companies the moral or ethical right. Social media companies deserve to be criticized, not for censorship per se but for doing so in a biased manner and for engaging in the practice when they hold monopolies on electronic communication. Monopolies violate federal law (the Sherman Anti-Trust Act).

A monopoly exists when a company gains exclusive control over a good or service in a specified market. Monopolies are illegal if they gain and maintain exclusive control through nefarious means meant to preclude competition or if they engage in what the courts call "exclusionary acts." This is where social media companies may be vulnerable. Censorship on the basis of political status or worldviews could be deemed an exclusionary act by the courts. In addition, efforts by the social media giants to prevent the establishment of competing platforms more friendly to Christian and conservative postings should certainly be viewed as attempts to preclude competition.

By censoring conservative and Christian postings and by putting up roadblocks to the establishment of competing platforms, social media companies may be guilty of maintaining exclusive control over electronic communication by dishonest means. If this is determined to be the case, they may have to revise their censorship practices or face being broken up by Congress on the basis of anti-trust legislation. This is not likely to happen in a Congress controlled by leftist ideologues who are happy to see conservatives and Christians censored. However, the reins of power in Congress go back and forth between political parties. In a Congress controlled by conservatives, the big tech companies controlling the largest social media platforms may find themselves facing anti-trust legislation.

In the meantime, the message Christians can convey in love to those who approve of social media censorship is this: Just because a private company has a right to do something does not mean it should. With every right comes a corresponding responsibility. In this case, social media companies have a moral obligation to be fair and balanced in deciding what postings are acceptable on their platforms. An appropriate question to ask those who support the biased approach social media companies take to censorship is this: How would you respond if the postings they censor were your postings instead of those of conservatives and Christians? Companies developing reputations for being unfair, biased, or unjust eventually fall victim to their own shortsighted, unethical policies.

DISAGREEING WITHOUT BEING DISAGREEABLE

The cancel culture is the quintessential example of handling disagreements in a disagreeable manner. For cancel-culture practitioners to be disagreeable when faced with differing opinions should surprise no one. After all, the ability to disagree with someone without being disagreeable is a sign of godly character. Those who reject God but accept sin are not likely to personify godly character. Nor are they likely to embrace His teachings. This is important because the ugliness associated with the cancel culture is a direct result of its practitioners rejecting God but accepting sin. The vilification, denigration, and defamation associated with the cancel culture are what human discourse uses when it lacks the tempering influence of Christ.

Believers, on the other hand, are called to treat others with respect, including those they disagree with. As Christians, we are to ever bear in mind that even the most disagreeable people were created by God and can be redeemed by God. Romans 14:1 admonishes us to welcome those who are weak in faith and to avoid quarreling over opinions with them. Consequently, the best course of action for Christians who are attacked for speaking God's truth—whether in person or on the internet—is to respond in ways reflecting the image of Christ. Doing so might just make you an instrument in salvaging the soul of someone who rejects the Lord.

To reflect the image of Christ when you interact with others, commit to telling the truth as set forth in Scripture even when recipients don't want to hear it and no matter how they respond to it. As a Christian, your responsibility is to convey God's truth. Opening the eyes, ears, and hearts of recipients is up to God. You cannot control how people respond to your postings on the internet, but you can control your responses to them. This is what God expects of you. Be tactful, loving, and humble in presenting your message and in choosing the words you use in your messages, but do not stray from God's truth.

As a Christian, you are still human. This means the temptation to respond in-kind to negative, angry, or insulting posts is always there. Don't do it. Instead, think of the message in Ephesians 4:15 where we read, "Rather, speaking the truth in love, we are to grow up in every way into him who is the head, into Christ." Every time we refuse to let another person's bad behavior cause us to respond similarly we grow in Christ. Equally important, every time we do this Satan is struck and there is the chance an unbeliever will be pointed to Christ by our example.

WHAT YOU CAN DO

To play a positive role in eliminating the cancel culture and anti-Christian censorship, begin by studying what the Bible has to say about this topic. Helpful verses for providing wise counsel to cancel-culture practitioners and their victims include the following:

• **Romans 12:2:** *"Do not be conformed to this world, but be transformed by the renewal of your mind, that by testing you may discern what is the will of God, what is good and acceptable and perfect."* This verse may help you make the point to victims of internet flaming that the views of the world need not be of concern to people who have Christ in their hearts. Being a child of God is the only affirmation any person needs or will ever need. People who have the affirmation of Christ do not need the affirmation of peers or anyone else.

- **John 15:19:** *"If you were of the world, the world would love you as its own; but because you are not of the world, but I chose you out of the world, therefore the world hates you."* This verse may help you provide wise counsel to people who are upset because they have been attacked, censored, or de-platformed by practitioners of the cancel culture. When anti-God unbelievers attack people, it means those people are being consistent Christians. The more hateful cancel-culture advocates become, the more effectively those they attack are serving Christ.

- **Colossians 2:8:** *"See to it that no one takes you captive by philosophy and empty deceit, according to human tradition, according to the elemental spirits of the world, and not according to Christ."* This verse may help you provide wise counsel to people who are tempted to give in to cancel-culture supporters to avoid being subjected to their wrath. The point to be made is this: it is better to be in accord with Christ than with the world.

- **2 Corinthians 6:14:** *"Do not be unequally yoked with unbelievers. For what partnership has righteousness with lawlessness. Or what fellowship has light with darkness?"* This verse may help you provide wise counsel to people who feel pressured to go along with anti-God proponents. Going along with those who reject God but accept sin is to allow yourself to be unequally yoked.

To speak the truth in love to victims of the cancel culture, you must first know the truth. Knowing what the Bible says about this issue will equip you to help people who are being flamed, canceled, censored, or de-platformed gain a positive perspective on what they are dealing with. The verses recommended herein are just to get you started. The Bible has much more to say about the machinations of the cancel culture.

Once you have studied what Scripture teaches about the cancel culture, pray God will comfort and strengthen people who are being flamed, canceled, or de-platformed by leftist ideologues. Pray, also, God will reach out to practitioners of the cancel culture and change their hearts. If you are not sure how to pray about this issue, recite the following prayer:

> *Lord, I am concerned about Christian brothers and sisters who are being canceled for speaking the truth of Your Word. Please wrap these victims in Your strong and loving arms and help them turn to You instead of the world for the approval and reassurance they need. Open their hearts to the light of Christ and close them to the darkness of the cancel culture. I also ask You to turn cancel-culture practitioners from the hate, anger, and conceit filling their hearts and infuse them with the love of Christ. It is in the holy name of Jesus I ask for Your intercession on behalf of cancel-culture victims and practitioners. Amen.*

When you have prayed for victims and practitioners of the cancel culture, the next step is to make sure your children and grandchildren know that being a child of Christ is ultimately the only approval and assurance they need in their lives. If we, as Christians, raise our children well, we can overcome the cancel culture in just one generation.

Having studied the Bible, prayed, and made sure your own children and grandchildren know that a personal relationship with Christ by far outshines the approval of the world, here are some other things you can do to help overcome the cancel culture:

- Refuse to be diverted from speaking biblical truths by those who reject God but accept sin and, as a result, seek to cancel you. Persevere in the faith no matter how vicious the attacks on you become. This is the message in Psalm 16:8 where David stated he would not be shaken because he kept the Lord always before him at his right hand. The truth can be suppressed for a time, but it eventually finds its way to the surface. Persevere knowing God's Word is the truth and it will prevail. If you become discouraged, think of the example in Jeremiah 38:14–23 where the prophet risked his life to speak God's truth to King Zedekiah.
- Seek the approval of God, not the world. As a child of God, you cannot be canceled. You can be criticized, vilified, defamed, censored,

and de-platformed, but compared to the loving acceptance of God, these things—as hurtful as they might seem in the moment—matter little, if at all, in the long run. Your life and your salvation are in the hands of God, not people who would cancel you because they disagree with your beliefs. Heed the example of Daniel who, in spite of the king's decree to the contrary, continued to pray to God (Dan. 6:10). As a Christian, you are under the authority of a loving God, not the pressure of peers or the approval of the world.

- Encourage your church to offer classes—especially for teenagers—teaching the lessons explained in this chapter. Teenagers use social media constantly. For many, it is their preferred and most frequently used form of communication. As a result, they are particularly susceptible to the bullying tactics of cancel-culture supporters. It is critical that youngsters in the church learn to seek approval from God rather than their peers and guidance from the Bible rather than the internet.
- Whether or not your church offers classes for teens on this subject, make sure you teach your own children and grandchildren to commit to speaking God's truth no matter how their peers might respond and to seek the approval of God rather than the approval of others.
- Share information about this issue with other Christians who might be struggling with the negativity and bullying tactics of cancel-culture adherents.

The negativity associated with the cancel culture has no place in a Christ-centered culture. People who love their neighbors as themselves don't try to cancel them over differing opinions. Be prepared to make this point when you speak the truth in love about this disreputable practice to people who engage in it as well as to those who are victims of it. Unbelievers who are offended by the cancel culture need to understand they cannot have it both ways. They cannot continue to reject God and expect there to be no consequences. The cancel culture is just one more tragic consequence befalling a nation rejecting God but accepting sin.

CHAPTER 10

DRUG AND ALCOHOL ABUSE

Do you not know that you are God's temple and that
God's spirit dwells in you? If anyone destroys God's temple,
God will destroy him. For God's temple is holy,
and you are that temple.

—1 Corinthians 3:16–17

Every year more than fourteen million people in America aged twelve and older struggle with an alcohol disorder. Almost twenty million people in the same age group battle a drug disorder. Many Americans battle addictions to both alcohol and drugs. More than 65,000 people in America die of drug overdoses every year. This number includes those who die from overdosing on illicit drugs as well as prescription opioids.[1] More than 10,000 people die every year from drunk-driving accidents.[2] If these statistics shock you, they should. They are tragic. That is the bad news. The good news is these tragic consequences of rejecting God but accepting sin are preventable, and you can play a role in preventing them.

For the most part, people who indulge in substance abuse are trying to fill voids in their hearts. They turn to pills, the bottle, or both in search of the peace, comfort, relief, courage, or assurance only God can give them. This is an important point for Christians to understand. If you are going to speak the truth in love to people who struggle with drug or alcohol addiction or their loved ones, you will need to know the extent of the problem in America and the reasons why people turn to drugs and alcohol in the first place.

DRUG ABUSE IN AMERICA: EXTENT OF THE PROBLEM

Chances are you know someone who struggles with drug abuse. If so, you are not alone. Most people know someone who misuses drugs. The individual in question might be a family member, friend, colleague, or neighbor. If the drug abuser you know is a loved one, friend, or colleague, their misuse of drugs affects you too. The negative effects of drug abuse are never confined to just the abuser. They can spread through a family, church, business, or neighborhood like a poisonous vapor. This is why as a Christian you must be prepared to speak God's truth in love to people who misuse drugs. When you point drug addicts to Christ, you are pointing them to the only true and lasting way out of their dilemma.

The extent of the drug abuse problem in America is shocking. Here are just a few facts about the size of the problem:[3]

- Almost 10 percent of all adults in America struggle with a drug disorder every year.
- The majority of people (74 percent) who struggle with drug addiction also struggle with alcohol abuse.
- Almost 4 percent of the adolescent population in America (ages 12–17) struggles with a drug disorder every year. This means one out of every twenty-five adolescents in America is a drug abuser.
- More than two million young adults (18–25) struggle with a drug disorder every year. Heroin use in this age group doubled over the past ten years.
- More than four million adults aged twenty-six or older struggle with a drug disorder every year.
- More than one million senior citizens (aged sixty-five or older) struggle with a substance abuse problem every year (substance abuse includes drugs and/or alcohol).

- Cocaine is a one of the most frequently misused illicit drugs. More than 950,000 Americans struggle with cocaine abuse every year.
- Heroin is another frequently misused illicit drug. More than 650,000 adults aged twelve or older struggle with heroin abuse every year. The largest at-risk group for heroin use consists of Caucasian males who reside in large cities and are aged 18–25.
- Prescription drugs consisting of pain relievers, tranquillizers, stimulants, and sedatives affect even more people in America than either illicit cocaine or heroin. Approximately 1.7 million American adults aged twelve or older suffer from a prescription drug disorder every year.

Although drug addiction is a problem of epidemic proportions in America, it is only half of the problem. Closely related to America's drug addiction problem and often overlapping it is the problem of alcohol abuse. The two go hand in hand because drug addicts often misuse alcohol and vice-versa.

ALCOHOL ABUSE IN AMERICA: EXTENT OF THE PROBLEM

Just as you probably know someone who struggles with drug abuse, you probably also know someone who struggles with alcohol abuse. You might work or go to church with someone who misuses alcohol. You might have a family member or friend who is an alcoholic. Just as drug abusers affect not just themselves but the people who love them, care for them, or work with them, alcohol abusers also affect the lives of others. The negative effects of alcohol abuse can spread through a family, church, business, or neighborhood like spilled ink staining everything it touches. This is why as a Christian you must be prepared to lovingly speak God's truth to people who misuse alcohol as well as those who love them, care for them, or work with them.

The size of the alcohol-abuse problem in America may surprise you. Here are just a few facts illustrating the extent of the problem annually:[4]

- More than fourteen million adults in America aged twelve and older struggle with alcohol abuse.

- There is an alcohol addiction in the family history of more than half of all American adults.
- Approximately 440,000 adolescents aged 12–17 struggle with alcohol abuse.
- Approximately ten million adults aged twenty-six and older struggle with alcohol abuse.
- More than 900,000 elderly people in America struggle with alcohol abuse.
- People addicted to alcohol are two times more likely to be addicted to heroin too.
- Approximately three million young adults aged 18–25 struggle with alcohol abuse.
- More than 10 percent of the children in America live with a parent who misuses alcohol.
- Alcoholics Anonymous (AA) has more than two million members worldwide in 175 countries.

There are 34,000 liquor stores in America generating more than $50 billion in annual revenue.[5] There are also more than 59,000 bars and nightclubs.[6] Add to these the restaurants and grocery stores licensed to sell beer, wine, and liquor and the numbers are staggering. Clearly, alcohol is part of the fabric of American society and access to it is open and convenient.

With this said, a caveat is in order. The cause of the alcohol-abuse problem in America resides in the hearts of people who misuse the substance not in the number of liquor stores and bars available to them. This is an important point to grasp if you are going to help the victims of alcohol abuse. It was disturbing that at the height of the COVID-19 pandemic some states closed churches while allowing liquor stores and bars to remain open. Clearly, elected officials in those states need to re-examine their priorities. A culture centered on Christ doesn't restrict church attendance while leaving liquor stores and bars open.

There is another even more important point: America's alcoholism problem will not be solved by shutting down liquor stores and bars. This may sound like a step in the right direction, at least on the surface, but doing so would be treating a symptom of the problem rather than the cause. The most effective way to solve the alcohol-abuse problem in

America is to help alcoholics fill the voids in their hearts with the love, peace, and sustaining grace of Jesus Christ. When they look to God for help in conquering their demons instead of a bottle of liquor or pills, only then will alcoholics be able to reclaim their lives.

DRUNK-DRIVING BANE IN AMERICA

One of the tragic consequences caused by alcohol abuse in America is the destruction caused by drunk driving. According to the National Highway Traffic Safety Administration, every day nearly thirty people die in drunk-driving incidents in America. This amounts to more than 10,000 people per year. Almost one-third of all traffic fatalities in the United States involve drunk drivers. The financial costs of drunk-driving accidents exceed $40 billion annually.[7] The emotional costs to loved ones of the victims cannot be measured in dollars and cents but they are even higher. For this reason, it is important for Christians to be well-informed about this problem and be willing to speak God's truth in love to people who drink and drive.

Maybe you've heard someone who is drinking and plans to drive say, "A few drinks won't hurt me." This statement is certainly high on the list of the ten biggest lies people tell themselves. It takes very little alcohol consumption to numb the senses, impair judgment, and interfere with one's ability to react quickly and properly. Here are a few facts about alcohol consumption you should know and be able to recite to people who think a few drinks won't hurt them:[8]

- Alcohol consumption affects the central nervous system and, in turn, impairs an individual's judgment and physical abilities. The higher the level of alcohol in the blood the greater the impairment. An individual's alcohol level is a ratio of the weight of alcohol present in a specific volume of blood. The ratio is called the "Blood Alcohol Concentration" or BAC.
- With a BAC of .08 grams of alcohol per deciliter of blood, a person's physical and judgmental impairment are sufficient to make driving dangerous. Concentration, short-term memory, speed control, and information-processing ability are all impaired at this level of alcohol consumption. Because of this fact, it is illegal to drive with a

BAC of .08 or higher. This law applies in all fifty states, the District of Columbia, and Puerto Rico.

- An individual's judgment and physical abilities can be impaired at BAC levels lower than .08. For example, in a typical year more than 1,500 people are killed in alcohol-related crashes involving drivers with BACs as low as .01. This is an important point to share with people who think driving after having a few drinks is acceptable.

People turn to alcohol and drugs for a lot of reasons. In doing so, they may be looking for good things, but they are looking in bad places. The temporary relief, comfort, courage, or thrills from engaging in substance abuse are bought at a high price, a price including broken relationships, lost jobs, shattered marriages, financial ruin, health problems, and even death. For this reason, Christians need to understand why people turn to drugs and alcohol. Explaining to substance abusers why their needs cannot be satisfied by a bottle of liquor or pills is an important part of speaking God's truth in love to them.

WHY PEOPLE TURN TO DRUGS AND ALCOHOL

If you understand why people turn to drugs and alcohol, you will be better equipped to cut through the fog of confusion, misdirection, and denial addicts often use to justify their choices. The word "choices" used here is important. Nobody forces people to misuse drugs and alcohol. Since misusing alcohol or drugs is a choice, people who choose to engage in substance abuse can also choose not to. Although it is true, it does not mean choosing to avoid drugs or alcohol is an easy choice. In fact, for some individuals, turning their backs on drugs or alcohol is the most difficult choice they will ever make. It is important to give substance abusers the support they need and to show them there is a better choice for coping with their demons.

People who misuse drugs and alcohol need to know they can choose God instead of substance abuse and doing so is the right choice. In fact, it is the only choice that will restore their lives and sustain them permanently. God can fill the void in their hearts and give purpose to their lives. This is where you come in. As a Christian, you can point them to Christ and share His truth with them. No matter how much counseling and rehabilitation they receive, they are not likely to restore their lives permanently unless and until their recovery is anchored in Christ. This is another of the hard truths you must be prepared to share in love with substance abusers.

The reasons people turn to drugs and alcohol vary from person to person. What follows are some of the more common reasons:[9]

- *Escape.* People who feel overwhelmed by life or the need to fill a void in their hearts often turn to drugs and alcohol. They might be dealing with stress, broken relationships, abuse, loneliness, grief, financial problems, job- or school-related pressures, family demands, feelings of failure, isolation, or a host of other emotional stressors. They see alcohol or drugs as offering temporary relief—a brief escape from the problems weighing them down. Here is a hard truth you may have to lovingly share with people in this category: when the bottle is empty and the pills are gone, the problems are still there, making them worse in the long run.

- *Enjoyment.* Some people turn to drugs or alcohol seeking enjoyment, thrills, or instant gratification. Abusers in this category may be bored or they may have timid personalities preventing them from participating fully in social activities. If the latter applies, they probably feel the sting of peer pressure for not participating. This just makes matters worse. For people in this category, alcohol and drugs serve as a form of courage in a bottle, a way to overcome inhibitions or to bolster themselves to seek new thrills. A hard truth you may have to lovingly share with people in this category is when the alcohol or pills wear off, the inhibitions and need for thrills or instant gratification will still be there. Alcohol- or drug-induced highs are temporary. Further, these temporary highs are never worth the permanent lows that follow. Artificial substitutes for quality of life always fail, and more and more is needed in the effort.

- *Relief.* Some people turn to alcohol and drugs because they suffer from chronic physical pain, emotional problems, or anxiety. For abusers in this category, alcohol and drugs are a form of self-medication. Alcohol and drugs can deaden physical pain temporarily, allow one to forget emotional problems for the moment, and make anxiety go away for a while. In all of these examples, alcohol and drugs bring welcome relief, at least in the short run. Unfortunately, the relief is temporary. Further, the more of these substances people use for relief, the more they need. Those who self-medicate using drugs or alcohol are traveling down a one-way street to disaster. Eventually, abusers in this category build up a tolerance to alcohol or drugs. As this happens, they require heavier and heavier doses to get the same effect. Eventually they reach a point where no amount of self-medication can bring the relief they seek.

- *Control.* Some people turn to alcohol and drugs because they tire of being under the control of an outside authority and want to rebel. The unwanted authority figure in question might be a parent, supervisor, guardian, teacher, coach, or anyone else in a position of authority. Because they tire of being expected to follow someone else's rules, substance abusers who seek control purposely choose behaviors breaking the rules by misusing drugs or alcohol. For people in this category, substance abuse is a form of rebellion. Misusing alcohol or drugs is a way of thumbing their noses at authority and taking control for themselves, or so they think. What they do not understand is that by turning to drugs or alcohol they are just substituting one form of control for another. In short order their lives will be controlled by alcohol or pills. All they have achieved is exchanging one master for another, and few masters are harder on those they control than alcohol and drugs.

The needs driving people to misuse alcohol or drugs are understandable. The problem is not so much in having these needs but in seeking to satisfy them with a chemical. People who do this are looking for help in the wrong places. As a Christian, you know the only source of lasting help for substance abusers is Jesus Christ. Consequently, your role in helping people who misuse alcohol and drugs is to point them to Christ.

COST OF ALCOHOL AND DRUG ABUSE IN AMERICA

The cost of substance abuse in America is immense. It can be measured in dollars and cents and in the toll taken on families, loved ones, and friends. Regardless how it is measured, the cost is staggering. The financial costs include healthcare, legal proceedings, related criminal activity, and loss of productivity on the job. Recent estimates put the cost of substance abuse—including alcohol and illegal drugs—at more than $740 billion a year, a number that continues to grow.[10]

Substance abuse drains more than $500 billion a year from the economy and from the budgets of individuals and families. Imagine all the good that money could do if it were put to positive uses. Yet as shocking as the financial costs of substance abuse are, they are dwarfed by the human costs—family stress, broken relationships, divorce, emotional trauma to children, loss of jobs, reduced quality of life, increased violence, child abuse, and even suicide.[11]

Substance abuse can damage families beyond repair. The emotional toll taken on spouses, children, and parents when there is a substance abuser in the home cannot be overstated. When a family member misuses alcohol or drugs, trust in that individual is broken, conflict becomes the norm, communicating with the abuser is difficult if not impossible, often aggressive behavior is introduced, and violence is common.

Children who witness a parent or older sibling abusing drugs or alcohol are more likely to develop substance abuse disorders themselves. They are also more likely to be neglected or abused physically or sexually. Children who witness arguments, physical altercations, and violent behavior from their parents not only undergo extreme emotional distress, they often adopt these behaviors themselves. Some children actually develop guilt complexes from observing this kind of behavior in their parents thinking they are the cause of it. The emotional stress a substance-abusing parent or older sibling causes children can inhibit their development and result in lifelong mental disorders.[12]

WHAT YOU CAN DO

To play a positive role in preventing substance abuse or in helping addicts escape it, begin by studying what the Bible has to say about this topic. Helpful verses for providing wise counsel to substance abusers or their loved ones include the following:

- **1 Peter 5:8:** *"Be sober-minded; be watchful. Your adversary the devil prowls around like a roaring lion, seeking someone to devour."* This verse may help you speak the truth in love about the dangers of drugs and alcohol to someone who misuses them. Alcohol and drugs are tools the devil uses to take control of people and ruin their lives. Individuals don't gain control of themselves or their lives by using drugs or alcohol, they lose control and they lose it to the evil one whose goal is to ruin them.

- **Proverbs 20:1:** *"Wine is a mocker, strong drink a brawler, and whoever is led astray by it is not wise."* This verse may help you speak the truth in love to someone who seeks refuge in a bottle of liquor. The alcohol they drink mocks them and allows them to be led astray by Satan.

- **1 Corinthians 15:33:** *"Do not be deceived: 'Bad company ruins good morals.'"* This verse may help you speak the truth in love to someone who is spending time with the wrong crowd, a crowd of drinkers and drug users. The message you can convey to people who are making this mistake is "Bad company ruins good morals." This, in turn, can ruin your life. People who tempt or pressure others to misuse alcohol or drugs don't care about them, but God does. Spending time in the company of the Holy Spirit rather than peers who encourage substance abuse is the better choice.

- **Matthew 6:13:** *"And lead us not into temptation, but deliver us from evil."* This portion of the Lord's Prayer from Matthew 6:13 may help you speak the truth in love to substance abusers who are allowing themselves to be tempted by alcohol or drugs or those who pressure them to use these substances. By turning their backs on drugs and alcohol, people you care about can deliver themselves from evil.

To speak the truth in love about substance abuse, you must first know the truth, and God's Word is the truth. Knowing what the Bible says about this issue will equip you to point the way to Christ for substance abusers. The verses recommended herein are just to get you started. The Bible has much more to say about the issue of substance abuse.

Once you have studied what Scripture teaches about substance abuse, pray God will intercede on behalf of those who misuse drugs and alcohol as well as those who love and care about them. If you are not sure how to pray about this issue, recite the following prayer:

> *Lord, I am concerned about (Joseph). He is clearly misusing drugs and alcohol. I fear he is seeking refuge from the problems weighing him down by turning to liquor and pills. Will You have mercy on (Joseph) and intercede in his life? Help him turn from substance abuse to You and fill the void in his heart with the love, strength, and reassurance only You can provide. Will You also comfort (Joseph's) family members and friends who care about him and show them how to help him? If it is Your will, help me play a positive role in turning (Joseph) from the path he is on to a path that leads to You. I lift up this prayer in the holy name of Jesus. Amen.*

When you have prayed for the person you are concerned about as well as for his or her family and friends, the next step is to make sure your children and grandchildren learn to place their troubles at the feet of Jesus Christ rather than turning to drugs or alcohol for relief. Teach them life in a fallen world is filled with ups and downs, but the Holy Spirit is always right next to them and available to help. If we, as Christians, raise our children right, we can reduce substance abuse substantially in just one generation.

Having studied the Bible, prayed, and made sure your children and grandchildren know a heart filled with Christ is far better than a body filled with alcohol or pills, here are some other things you can do to help prevent alcohol and drug abuse:

- Inform yourself and others about the problem of substance abuse with the information in this chapter as well as from other sources. Use this information when you speak the truth in love to people who misuse alcohol or drugs or when you talk with their family members and friends. What you have to say may not be welcomed by substance abusers, at least not at first, but it is essential they hear it anyway. You never know when God might open their eyes, ears, and hearts to what you have told them.

- Approach those who misuse alcohol and drugs out of love—not anger, frustration, or bitterness. You won't be able to point substance abusers to Christ if you make them defensive, and pointing them to Christ is the best way to help them.
- Encourage your church to confront this issue openly. Urge your pastor to preach on the subject of substance abuse and to ask recovering addicts to speak to the congregation about their experiences. Embrace people in your church or community who are struggling with substance abuse rather than condemning them. Condemnation and rejection will just magnify the problem of drug and alcohol abuse. Encourage your church to provide face-to-face counseling for substance abusers and their family members. If your church is too small to afford a biblical counseling center, establish a relationship with one in a larger church and make referrals. Make sure the counseling services are open to church members and non-church members alike.
- Encourage your church to provide instruction on responsible behavior relating to drinking and driving (e.g., never drink and drive, if you host a party where alcohol is served make sure your guests are sober when they leave or have a designated driver to take them home, do not let someone you know who has been drinking get behind the wheel of a car, etc.). Never assume people in your congregation don't drink to excess or teens in your church won't be pressured by their peers to. Use instruction and wise counsel to prevent drunk driving.
- Make sure your church doesn't overlook the children of substance abusers. Provide counseling, instruction, and support for them too or make referrals to churches or organizations that can. The children of substance abusers are often the worst victims of this scourge.
- Encourage your church leaders to partner with other churches and organizations providing services to help substance abusers and their family members. Make sure your church can either provide direct services to children of substance abusers or has a partnership with another church or organization that can.
- Make preventing substance abuse and drunk driving part of your church's youth program. It is less costly, less time-consuming, and more effective to prevent these problems than to treat them.

Substance abuse will be much less of a problem in a Christ-centered culture. Be prepared to make this point when you speak God's truth in love to people who struggle with this problem. When Christ enters an individual's heart, the unmet needs that lead to substance abuse don't necessarily go away but the person in question now has a healthy and lasting way to deal with them. Instead of seeking relief, courage, or comfort in a bottle of liquor or pills, the individual in question can now seek these things in the loving arms of Christ.

In addition to making this point to substance abusers, be prepared to make it to unbelievers who express concerns about substance abuse. People who reject God but accept sin need to understand they cannot have it both ways. They cannot push God out of their lives and out of the culture and expect there to be no consequences. Substance abuse is just one more tragic consequence suffered by a nation that rejects God but accepts sin. Consequently, curtailing substance abuse begins with embracing Christ.

CHAPTER 11

CORRUPTION: LYING, CHEATING, AND STEALING

*By which he has granted to us his precious and very great
promises, so that through them you may become partakers of
the divine nature, having escaped from the corruption that is
in the world because of sinful desire.*

—2 Peter 1:4

It should come as no surprise that rejecting God but accepting sin results in a culture of darkness, depravity, and corruption or that such a culture encourages lying, cheating, and stealing. Corruption is fraudulent or dishonest behavior, often by people in positions of authority, although corruption it is not limited to authority figures. In a fallen world, any person can be corrupted by the influence of Satan. Consequently, unless a nation's culture is centered on Christ, there will be people at all levels of society who will lie, cheat, and steal. This is precisely what is happening in America and around the world today.

The corruption from rejecting God but accepting sin reveals itself in a number of ways including corporate ethics scandals, fraudulent transactions, income-tax evasion, identity theft, influence peddling, money laundering, embezzlement, extortion, nepotism, theft, robbery, burglary, bribery scandals, and cheating, to name just a few examples. When individuals or a nation reject God, they also reject His Word. In fact, anyone who rejects the Bible rejects God because He reveals Himself to us through His Word. This results in predictable but tragic consequences, one of which is widespread corruption.

The book of Exodus (chapter 20) contains God's Ten Commandments. The Eighth Commandment forbids stealing. It also forbids cheating which is a form of stealing. The Ninth Commandment forbids lying. The Greatest Commandment, as stated by Jesus Christ in Matthew 22:37–38, admonishes us to love God with all our hearts and to love our neighbors as ourselves. Hence, the Greatest Commandment forbids all forms of corruption. Perhaps this is one of the reasons Christ called it the "Greatest Commandment"; it prohibits all forms of iniquity, depravity, and corruption.

When it comes to obeying the Greatest Commandment, you do not demonstrate love for God or your neighbors by lying, cheating, or stealing. You do not demonstrate love by engaging in corrupt acts detrimental to your neighbors or any of God's children. Corruption occurs because people reject God and His Word. If people committed themselves to obeying God's Commandments, corruption and all of the various sins associated with it would soon disappear.

Because of widespread corruption by individuals in positions of authority, many Americans no longer trust their government, banks, businesses, hospitals, school systems, colleges, or each other. According to a Gallop poll, 60 percent of Americans believe corruption exists on a broad scale among businesses and only about 20 percent trust banks.[1] When the honesty and integrity of a nation's institutions are doubted, trust breaks down and the lack of trust spreads. Before long, individual citizens begin to ask themselves, "If everyone else is going to lie, cheat, and steal, why shouldn't I?"

People who doubt the integrity of a nation's institutions soon question why they should be honest with those institutions. "If the government isn't honest with me, why should I be honest with the government when I file my income taxes?" "If my teachers cheat on their recertification exams, why shouldn't I cheat on the tests they give me?" "If the CEO of my insurance company was arrested for fraud, why shouldn't

I file a fraudulent claim with the company?" Corruption and mistrust beget more corruption and mistrust. Unless the situation is turned around, the downward spiral continues until the problem spins out of control. This is why it is so important for Christians to do their part to curtail corruption by encouraging trust in God rather than the world.

LYING IN AMERICA

Even in a Christ-centered culture, lying still occurs, but it is frowned on and deemed unacceptable as a violation of the Ninth Commandment. It is something to repent of and atone for. But in a godless culture, lying is not just common, it is expected, tolerated, and even deemed acceptable in some instances. In today's culture, people lie about their age, profession, income taxes, marital status, golf scores, grades, health, intentions, schedules, education, work experience, finances, and a host of other things. Lying on résumés, for example, has become so common employers are forced to conduct time-consuming, costly background checks on job applicants to separate fact from fiction.

In a godless culture, lying becomes a way of life. For example, how often have you found yourself struggling with an issue but answered "Nothing" when asked, "What's wrong?" How often have you felt bad physically or emotionally and yet answered "I'm fine" when asked, "Are you okay?" If you do not want to talk about what is bothering you or how you feel, an honest answer to the first question would be, "I am dealing with a difficult situation, but would rather not discuss it now." An honest answer to the second question would be, "I don't feel well, but we have more important things to discuss." To say nothing is wrong when, in fact, something is wrong or to say "I'm fine" when, in fact, you are not fine is lying. The lie may be well intended but it's still a lie nonetheless.

Another example of a commonly told lie occurs when you bump into an old friend or colleague you haven't seen in a while and say, "It's great to see you—I'll call you so we can get together sometime." In reality, you have no plans to call your friend or get together in the future. The promise was just a way to end the conversation comfortably so you could get on with more pressing matters. If you had no intention of calling the individual in question, a more honest way to end the conversation would have been, "It was nice to see you again. I hope all goes well for you."

How widespread is lying in America? The following statistics put the issue into perspective:[2]

- By the age of four, 90 percent of children have learned to lie.
- Americans tell an average of eleven lies per week.
- In a ten-minute conversation, American adults tell an average of three lies.
- Thirteen percent of patients admit they lie to their physician.
- Thirty percent of Americans lie about diet and exercise.
- American men tell six lies a day to their partner, boss, or colleagues.
- American women tell three lies a day to their partner, boss, or colleagues.
- Seventy percent of liars admit they would tell the same lies again.
- Ninety percent of middle-schoolers admit they cheat on their homework.

If you find these statistics disturbing, you should. Lying has become a canker on American society, an unfortunate but imbedded aspect of the culture. America has become a country where lying has become so common that in many cases it is accepted or, at the very least, tolerated. When lying becomes common practice, people just assume they are being lied to. As a result, trust in people, organizations, authority figures, and a nation's institutions is undermined. When people cannot trust each other or the organizations and institutions they depend on, society begins to break down. This fact underscores why it is important for individual Christians to commit to doing their part to reclaim the culture for Christ.

WHY DO PEOPLE LIE?

People lie for a number of reasons, most of them understandable but all of them wrong. The reasons people give most frequently for lying are as follows:[3]

- To avoid embarrassment
- To avoid guilt

- To avoid confrontation or conflict
- To get their way or to prevail in an argument
- To avoid hurting someone else's feelings
- To make themselves look better

Lying to Avoid Embarrassment

Alumni who attend class reunions sometimes lie about their lives since graduation to avoid the embarrassment of being viewed by their peers as failures or underachievers. Students sometimes lie about their grades to avoid the embarrassment of poor performance. Colleagues sometimes lie about their salaries to avoid the embarrassment of making less money. High-school students sometimes claim to be sick to avoid the embarrassment of not being asked to the Junior-Senior Prom. Hundreds of situations tempt people to lie as a way to avoid embarrassment.

Although wishing to avoid embarrassment is an understandable motive, lying is still lying. Regardless the motive, it amounts to purposefully deceiving others. In the long run telling the truth is better. This is the message in 1 Peter 3:10 where we read: "Whoever desires to love life and see good days, let him keep his tongue from evil and his lips from speaking deceit." Those who lie, even if the motive is to avoid embarrassment, are more likely to see bad days than good. Lies have a way of coming back to bite you, often at the worst possible times.

Lying is not excused because the motive is understandable. Being understandable doesn't make one's motive acceptable. Consequently, a hard truth to share with people who lie to avoid embarrassment is *they are worrying too much about what other people think of them and too little about what God thinks of them.* God is not pleased when people lie. Those who lie to avoid embarrassment may fool the people they lie to, but they don't fool God. It's better to be embarrassed in the eyes of one's peers for telling the truth than to displease God by lying.

Lying to Avoid Guilt

One of the most frequently told lies is, "I didn't do it." Criminals tell this lie in an attempt to avoid prosecution. Cheating spouses tell this lie to avoid admitting infidelity. Children tell this lie to avoid parental discipline. Students tell this lie to avoid being punished for cheating. Employees tell this lie to avoid the consequences of violating company policies. Business executives tell this lie to avoid being unmasked in corporate-fraud scandals. Politicians tell this lie to avoid negative publicity when they are caught up in scandals.

A hard truth to share in love with people who lie to avoid guilt comes from Proverbs 19:9: *"A false witness will not go unpunished, and he who breathes out lies will perish."* When they lie to avoid guilt and the corresponding consequences, people think they are getting away with their indiscretions, but they aren't. Even if the person they lie to is fooled, God isn't—and His judgment of unrepentant sinners will be worse than any earthly punishment might have been.

No matter what sins may have been committed, it is better in the long run to tell the truth from the outset. Telling one lie to avoid guilt often creates the need to tell more lies. In such cases, it is not long before liars spin such a complicated web of deceit they can no longer keep their lies straight. They invariably fall prey to their own fabrications. When this happens, they are guilty of not just the original offense but the subsequent lies they told to avoid guilt. In fact, the lies they told to avoid guilt often amount to a worse offense than what they lied about in the first place.

Lying to Avoid Confrontations or Conflict

Some people are so averse to confrontation and conflict they will lie to avoid them. People can be averse to confrontation for a number of reasons. They might be leery because of what resulted from a blow-up during a confrontation in the past, fear of being wrong and made to look foolish, a lack of confidence, or reluctance to hurt someone else's feelings. Some Christians shy away from confrontations because they confuse the biblical admonition to be meek with being timid. This is a mistake. Timidity is a product of insecurity. Meekness, on the other hand, is inner strength willingly and purposefully kept under control. Jesus was meek but He was certainly not timid.

As for avoiding conflict, fear is the most common reason people give. Some people avoid conflict out of fear of damaging a relationship. Others fear the potential negative consequences that might come from the conflict, consequences such as retribution. Some people are afraid conflict might escalate and become physical and are intimidated by physical violence. Others fear they might lose their temper and do or say something they will later regret.

While all these reasons are understandable, they don't make lying to avoid confrontations or conflict right. God condemns lying regardless of the reason. This is why in Psalm 34:13 He tells His children to "Keep your tongue from evil and your lips from speaking deceit." Rather than lie to avoid confrontation or conflict, a better response is to practice disagreeing without being disagreeable, sharpening one's communication skills, learning to be tactful, and, most important, becoming an attentive, perceptive listener.

A hard truth to share in love with people who lie to avoid confrontation or conflict is this: *it is better in the long run to tell the truth about ideas, recommendations, or plans you disagree with than to appear to approve of them.* If your silence makes you appear to approve of something and it doesn't work out, you become complicit in its failure. Truthfully and tactfully stating your disagreement is always better than lying to avoid a confrontation or conflict. You do not want to see someone stumble or make a serious mistake because you were afraid to point out the problems with his or her idea or plans.

Lying to Get One's Way or to Prevail in an Argument

The need to get one's way in all cases or to prevail in an argument over an issue that does not really matter is based in selfishness, and selfishness is a sin. The opposite of selfishness is selflessness. People with Christ in their hearts know the value of selflessness. Philippians 2:3, among many other verses in the Bible, provides guidance on this topic: "Do nothing from rivalry or conceit, but in humility count others more significant than yourselves." People who heed this verse from Scripture are less likely to lie to get their own way or to prevail in an argument. They know doing so is a manifestation of selfishness.

A hard truth to share in love with people who are willing to lie to get their way or to needlessly prevail in an argument is this: *getting your way in every instance and needlessly prevailing in an argument are not worth the price you may eventually pay.* People who get a reputation for always demanding their own way or always needing to prevail in an argument often lose credibility and respect in the eyes of others. When this happens, their views are ignored making it difficult to get their way or prevail in an argument even when they happen to be right.

Lying to Avoid Hurting Someone's Feelings

Wanting to avoid hurting someone's feelings is commendable, but lying to achieve this laudable goal is wrong. A hard truth to share in love with people who think telling "a little white lie" to avoid hurting someone's feelings is this: *if you care enough about people to protect their feelings, you care enough to tell them the truth.* You don't show people you care by lying to them. Better to tactfully tell the truth than to lie.

When people lie to avoid hurting someone's feelings, chances are the lie will eventually be revealed. This is the message in Luke 8:17 where we read: "For nothing is hidden that will not be made manifest, nor is anything secret that will not be known and come to light." The truth is a stubborn thing. No matter how hard people try to hide it or suppress it, the truth usually finds its way out of the darkness and into the light. When this happens, a lie that was told to avoid hurting someone's feelings will often hurt more than the truth would have—especially if the truth was told with tact.

In addition to the admonition about lying contained in the Ninth Commandment, there are practical reasons for telling the truth, even when the truth might hurt. The first is the impact lying can have on a relationship. Human relationships are built on trust, and nothing undermines trust faster than lying, even when the lies are told with good intentions. When people are lied to, regardless the reason, they find it difficult to trust the person who lied. Without trust there can be no communication, and communication is the glue holding relationships together.

Lying to Make Yourself Look Better

To make themselves look better, people sometimes lie about such things as their age, weight, income, grades, experience, education, family tree, past, and a host of other things. People who lie for this reason are trying to impress others or they are looking for their approval, both of which are mistakes. A hard truth to share in love with people who lie to make themselves look better is *staking one's self-esteem on the approval of others is a mistake.* Giving too much credence to the approval of friends, peers, colleagues, or other people is a mistake.

Peer approval is usually conditional and almost always fleeting. It can be here today and gone tomorrow. This is because too often it is based on what you can do for your peers rather than true admiration. For example, the star quarterback and big man on campus when the team is winning becomes a goat when the team starts losing. It wasn't that his fellow students admired him as an individual when the team was winning. Rather, they liked how he made them feel like winners by association. They were living their lives vicariously through him. When he no longer gave them good feelings about themselves, he lost their approval. Peer approval is like this. It is based less on the qualities of the individuals who are seeking approval than on the self-interest of peers who temporarily grant approval.

For this reason, it is important for Christians to point people who seek peer approval to Christ. When people give their hearts to Christ, His is the only approval they will ever need. This is the message in Galatians 1:10: "For am I now seeking the approval of man, or of God? Or am I trying to please man? If I were still trying to please man, I would not be a servant of Christ." Unlike peer approval, Christ's approval is genuine and not fleeting. Ask people who seek peer approval this question: Would you rather have the approval of someone who loved you so much He was willing to die a painful, horrible death to save you or someone who just wants what you can do for him in the here and now?

Lying has become part of the culture in America. It occurs with a shocking casualness and frequency and in many cases hardly raises eyebrows when it is discovered. Politicians caught in lies simply shrug the situation off and temporize by engaging in semantic subterfuge. Rather than admit to lying, the guilty parties claim they "misspoke." Worse yet, they get away with it. Too few people on either side of the television camera think to question what it means to "misspeak."

A lot of Americans are willing to accept lying as a normal part of social discourse. Nevertheless, lying is taking a toll on society. The more we are lied to, the more numb we become to lying. As we grow more accustomed to lying and being lied to, the cultural objections to lying are diminished. This, in turn, encourages more lying and the downward moral spiral accelerates. The result of this downward spiral is a culture in which nobody trusts anybody or anything. This is what a culture without Christ at its center looks like, and it's not a pretty picture—just look around.

CHEATING IN AMERICA

Cheating, like stealing, violates the Eight Commandment, but without Christ at the center of the culture, cheating becomes commonplace. In a culture devoid of Christ, cheating is just another way to achieve a goal, satisfy a need, ensure a result, or gain an advantage. To cheat is to knowingly act in a dishonest or unfair manner for the purpose of personal gain. Students cheat on assignments and exams, athletes cheat in sports contests, citizens cheat on their income taxes, spouses cheat on each other, gamblers cheat at card games, businesses cheat customers, and customers cheat businesses. Even little children learn to cheat in playground games. There is a popular bumper sticker that reads, "If you aren't cheating you aren't trying."

Cheating has become so prevalent that colleges and universities are forced to purchase expensive computer software for detecting plagiarism. Many students cheat by downloading essays and other writing assignments from the internet rather than doing their own work. Teachers and professors have to collect smart phones from students before administering tests because students will look up the correct answers to test questions. There are hundreds of websites at which cheating students who are willing to pay the fee can have essays and term papers written for them on virtually any subject.

Cheating is a form of stealing because it involves dishonestly gaining something of value. This being the case, it is prohibited by the Eighth Commandment as well as numerous other biblical admonitions. Cheating has reached such epidemic proportions in America it would be no exaggeration to claim our country has developed a cheating culture. Cheating scandals are now so common in sports, business, politics, education, healthcare, and most other fields of endeavor it sometimes appears cheating has become a way of life in America. For the sake of illustration, let's look at few examples of well-known cheating scandals.

Several years ago, the Houston Astros were caught cheating in order to win baseball games. The team devised a sophisticated system for stealing their opponent's pitching signals. The system allowed Houston's batters to know what pitch to expect even before the pitcher released the ball. This foreknowledge gave hitters an illegal advantage over the pitcher.

A batter in baseball is not supposed to know what pitch is coming until the pitcher releases the ball. Pitchers go to great lengths to conceal their pitches from batters. Batters, on the other hand, work hard to learn how to anticipate what pitch to expect in a given situation. The better hitters are the ones who become adept at anticipating the next pitch. This cat-and-mouse game between pitcher and batter is a fundamental and important part of baseball. Anything that gives a batter or a pitcher an illegal advantage undermines the integrity of the game.

Another example of cheating occurred when Rosie Ruiz won the Boston Marathon in record time one year. She accomplished this commendable feat not by training hard and giving her best effort, but by cheating. Instead of running the whole race, Ruiz hopped a ride on the subway, riding until she was about a mile from the finish line. There she got off and ran the last mile, winning in record time. Ruiz was caught in her scheme by a freelance photographer who happened to be on the subway with her.

Lance Armstrong became an idol to bicyclists worldwide by winning an unprecedented seven Tour de France titles, but his image was sullied when it turned out he cheated by using performance-enhancing drugs. After years of denying the fact, Armstrong finally admitted to cheating. As a result, he had to surrender his titles and was banned from professional cycling.

Track star Marion Jones, who won five Olympic medals, suffered the same fate for the same reason: using performance-enhancing drugs. She, too, initially denied cheating. Jones was not only stripped of her medals, she spent six months in prison for lying to federal prosecutors about using drugs. This was one of those cases in which the lie told to cover wrongdoing was worse than the original infraction.

The world of politics has also provided numerous instances of cheating. In 2020 what became known as the "Congressional Insider Trading Scandal" rocked the United States Senate when it appeared several senators violated the STOCK Act. This law prohibits the use of confidential information gained by government officials and employees from being used for profit. In short, the STOCK Act outlaws insider trading by government officials.

Just before the outbreak of the COVID-19 pandemic, senators received advanced warning of what was coming. Immediately thereafter, several of them sold stocks in companies potentially losing value because of the pandemic and bought stock in companies possibly increasing in value because of it. These transactions resulted in an insider trading investigation by the U.S. Department of Justice. Little came of the investigation. Nonetheless, the publicity surrounding it scandalized the U.S. Senate and further undermined the trust of American citizens in Congress and our justice system.

Members of Congress are privy to some of the most confidential and guarded information there is. They are supposed to be good stewards of that information and treat it ethically on behalf of American citizens. As stewards of information affecting the daily lives of American citizens, members of Congress must act in ways that engender trust. This is the message in 1 Corinthians 4:2 where we read: "Moreover, it is required of stewards that they be found faithful." Few things undermine trust faster than cheating or even the appearance of it.

Even education is not exempt from the sting of cheating scandals. Because of declining student performance, public school systems nationwide began requiring the administration of standardized tests as a way to hold teachers accountable. In most states, schools with high composite test scores on standardized tests are awarded various incentives while schools with low scores lose out. In 2015, a total of 178 educators from the Atlanta Public School System were charged with illegally tampering with test scores to falsely show improved performance. They corrected answers students gave on standardized exams to improve test scores.

After inquiries by the Georgia Bureau of Investigation, all but twelve of these educators admitted to cheating to enhance the scores of students on standardized tests. Those twelve educators chose to go to trial. Eleven of the twelve were convicted of racketeering and received fines, prison terms, or both. All 178 of the educators implicated in the cheating scandal would have benefitted from heeding the message in Proverbs 10:9: "Whoever walks in integrity walks securely, but he who makes his ways crooked will be found out."

There are hundreds of other examples of cheating scandals we could cite, but they all render the same conclusion: people can become so focused on a self-serving goal they are willing to do anything to achieve it, including cheating. In all of these cases, it would have been wise for the individuals involved to heed the warning in Luke 8:17: "For nothing is hidden that will not be made manifest, nor is anything secret that will not be known and come to light."

STEALING IN AMERICA

Stealing involves taking or using another person's property without permission. The temptation to steal is as old as mankind. This is why God included a prohibition against stealing in the Ten Commandments. The Eighth Commandment states clearly, "You shall not steal" (Exod. 20:15). Not surprisingly, stealing is a practice commonly associated with a culture devoid of Christ. The fact a lot of people reject God but accept sin is why stealing is so prevalent in American society today.

As a perfect illustration of accepting sin, San Francisco recently reduced the penalty for shoplifting to a misdemeanor in their city when $950 or less is stolen.[4] This bastion of lawlessness is not the only city in America to wink at lawbreakers.

Stealing can take several different forms including robbery, theft, shoplifting, fraud, and embezzlement. These examples are all traditional forms of stealing. As the culture has declined, stealing in all its manifestations has increased. For example, the number of home invasions occurring every year has increased as thieves seek the money needed to support their illegal drug trade or to steal prescription drugs. The traditional forms of stealing most likely to affect you are home invasions and automobile break-ins.

As despicable as the traditional forms of stealing are, there is an even more insidious form—one dwarfing all the others combined— identity theft. It is bad enough to steal someone's possessions, but to steal a person's identity takes the concept of theft to whole new depth of evil. Because of the internet, you are more likely to experience identity theft than a home invasion or automobile break-in. Hence, the remainder of this section on stealing focuses on identity theft.

Identity Theft in America

Identity theft involves stealing a person's identification data and using it for criminal purposes. The information stolen might be a driver's license number, employee identification number, credit card number, or some other form of identification unique to a given individual. The big prize for identity thieves is a victim's social security number. An identity thief can use a victim's social security number for a wide range of criminal activities.

The most common use of stolen identities is financial fraud— typically applying for loans or credit cards in the victim's name—but there are several other ways to illegally use someone's identity for personal gain. For example, an individual's identity might be used to obtain a false identification card, passport, or even a college transcript. Identity thieves even use stolen identification data to divert income-tax refunds from the legal recipients to themselves. A growing form of this insidious form of stealing is medical identity theft. Medical identity theft involves stealing a person's insurance information and using it to secure medical care or to charge insurance companies for unprovided medical care.

Identity theft costs Americans more than $56 billion a year, which exceeds the cost of all other forms of stealing combined.[5] More than 49 million people became victims of identity theft in 2020.[6] It is now commonplace for businesses and other kinds of organizations to be forced to announce identity thieves have defeated their security measures and gained access to thousands of customer records. This phenomenon is known as a data breach.

How common are data breaches? The year-to-date total of data breaches in 2021 has already exceeded 2020—1,291 times giving hackers access to approximately 281 million personal records.[7] Hackers who steal the data of large organizations use the information gained for their own purposes and then sell it to other identity thieves on the black market. This is why protecting citizens from identity theft has become a growth industry in America.

WHAT YOU CAN DO ABOUT CORRUPTION

To play a positive role in reducing corruption, begin by studying what the Bible has to say on this topic. Helpful verses for providing wise counsel to people who think lying, cheating, and stealing are acceptable include the following:

- **Proverbs 19:9:** *"A false witness will not go unpunished, and he who breathes out lies will perish."* This verse may help you provide wise counsel to someone who thinks lying is acceptable. The Bible is clear that liars will be punished and will even perish. An implicit message in this verse is liars will eventually be caught. Also unstated in this verse is no one ever gets away with lying because God knows even if the world doesn't.
- **Proverbs 10:9:** *"Whoever walks in integrity walks securely, but he who makes his ways crooked will be found out."* This verse may help you provide wise counsel to someone who thinks it's okay to cheat. An important part of the message is cheaters will be caught sooner or later. When that happens, the negative consequences will probably outweigh whatever temporary benefit was gained from cheating. Further, not only will cheaters "be found out," they already have been. God knows when someone cheats even if no one else does.
- **Proverbs 20:17:** *"Bread gained by deceit is sweet to a man, but afterwards his mouth will be full of gravel."* This verse may help you provide wise counsel to someone who thinks stealing is no big deal. It makes the point that the things gained from stealing might seem pleasing at first, but they will eventually cause regret, especially when the stealer is caught. Once again, in the eyes of an all-seeing God, stealers were caught the minute they committed their dishonest act.

- **2 Peter 2:19:** *"They promise them freedom, but they themselves are slaves of corruption. For whatever overcomes a person, to that he is enslaved."* This verse may help you provide wise counsel to someone about corruption in general, including lying, cheating, and stealing. It shows how corruption makes people into slaves. Corrupt people are never free because they must always worry about their lying, cheating, and stealing being revealed. Freedom comes only from the truth.

To speak the truth in love about corruption to people who think it is acceptable to lie, cheat, and steal, you must first know the truth, and God's Word is the truth. Knowing what the Bible says about the corruption of lying, cheating, and stealing will equip you to point the way to Christ for people who have chosen this path. The verses above are just to get you started. The Bible has much more to say about all forms of the rot of sin.

Once you have studied what Scripture teaches about corruption in all of its forms, pray God will replace the depravity in the hearts of those who lie, cheat, and steal with a commitment to honesty and integrity. Also pray God will help you be an effective instrument in pointing those who are corrupt to Christ. If you are not sure how to pray about this issue, recite the following prayer:

> *Lord, I am concerned about (Susan). She is so wrapped up in selfishness that lying, cheating, and stealing to get what she wants are acceptable to her. I pray You intercede on her behalf and replace the selfishness leading her down the wrong path with a commitment to honesty and integrity as defined in Scripture. I also pray You help her see the error of her ways and help me point her to Christ before her life is ruined by the misguided choices she is making. I ask for Your intercession on (Susan's) behalf in the holy name of Jesus. Amen.*

When you have prayed for the people you are concerned about, the next step is to ensure your children and grandchildren are taught the importance of honesty and integrity. Young people who learn to emulate the selflessness of Jesus Christ are not likely to grow up to lead lives of corruption. If we, as Christians, raise our children well, we can reduce corruption substantially in just one generation.

Having studied the Bible, prayed, and made sure your own children and grandchildren know the importance of living lives of integrity, here are some other things you can do to reduce the tragic consequences of rejecting God but accepting sin. Begin by knowing how to protect yourself from the more traditional forms of stealing such as home invasions and automobile break-ins. Then share this information with others and encourage your church to work with insurance companies or the local police department to sponsor seminars for church members and the community teaching the following simple tips about preventing home invasions:[8]

- Use bright lighting all around the outside of your home at night and leave several interior lights on when you are gone.
- Never let your home look empty when you are gone. Leave a television or radio on in addition to several interior lights.
- Never leave expensive items in your yard that might attract the attention of home invaders.
- Never hide a spare key under the doormat or any other obvious location where a home invader might find it.
- Beef up your windows, doors, and garage door. Flimsy points of entry invite the attention of home invaders.
- Use blinds and/or curtains to cover your windows. Never give home invaders the ability to see inside your home.
- Check your yard for blind spots affording home invaders places to hide without being seen by neighbors or passers-by. If you have blind spots, eliminate them.
- Keep your garage door closed. An open garage door is an open invitation to a home invader.
- Have a home security system installed.

To prevent automobile break-ins, observe the following tips, share them with others, and encourage your church to work with insurance companies or the local police department to sponsor seminars for church members and the community teaching the following simple tips:[9]

- Always lock your car doors and roll up the windows when you are out of your car. Many automobile break-ins do not require the perpetrators to actually break in because the car's owner left the doors unlocked.
- Never leave valuables in sight in your car. Most automobile break-ins are done by smash-and-grab opportunists who see something in a car they want.
- Turn on the car's security system if it has one.
- Use window tinting to the extent allowed by local laws to make it more difficult for would-be burglars to see what is in your car.
- Use steering lock mechanisms to discourage would-be car thieves.
- Never lock valuables in the glove box; it is too easy to break the lock.
- Put your valuables in the trunk before you get to your destination, especially parking lots. Would-be criminals often watch parking lots to see who puts valuables in their trunks. The locks on trunks can be easily defeated by an experienced car burglar.
- Be careful about where you park. If a neighborhood or area feels wrong or suspicious, park somewhere else.

To prevent identity theft, observe the following tips yourself, share them with others, and encourage your church to work with identity-theft experts to sponsor seminars for church members and the community teaching the following tips:[10]

- If you notice suspicious charges on credit or debit cards, notify your credit-card company immediately to cancel the cards and provide you with replacements.
- Never respond to emails, telephone calls, or letters in the mail asking for personal information. Also, never click on links appearing in unsolicited emails and never reveal your username or password to anyone.
- Change your username and password periodically.
- Request a security freeze with the three major credit bureaus. This will help prevent identity thieves from opening bank accounts or securing credit cards in your name.

- Sign up for online access to your bank accounts so you can monitor them daily rather than waiting for a monthly statement.
- Sign up with the three major credit bureaus for free credit reports.
- Report fraud immediately to your bank and to the police.
- Install identity-theft protection software including a firewall on your computer.

Encourage your church to be especially attentive to providing seminars covering the recommendations contained herein for elderly members of the congregation and community. Elderly people are often the targets of home invaders, car thieves, scammers, hackers, and identity thieves.

There is no place for stealing in any of its manifestations in a Christ-centered culture. As you interact with people inside and outside of your church, set an example of honesty and integrity that is the antithesis of lying, cheating, and stealing. Talk with young people you know and teach them corruption of all types is wrong. Speak the truth in love about corruption with people who reject God but are put off by the home invasions, car burglaries, and identity theft so prevalent in today's culture. Remind them they cannot have it both ways. They cannot continue to reject God, accept sin, and expect there to be no consequences. Corruption is one more example of what happens in a nation that rejects God but accepts sin.

CHAPTER 12

ROAD RAGE AND SIDELINE RAGE

Refrain from anger, and forsake wrath! Fret not yourself;
it tends only to evil.

—Psalm 37:8

Did you ever think the time would come when people would shoot each other over minor inconveniences such as driving too slowly, failing to respond quickly enough to a green light, or wanting the same parking space? Did you ever think the time would come when fathers and mothers would violently attack coaches, game officials, and other parents during their children's sports events and do it in front of their children?

Though it is difficult to believe it, these things are happening in America. In fact, appalling incidents such as these have become common in today's culture. The former concept is known as *road rage*, the latter as *sideline rage*. Both are examples of what happens when people reject God but accept sin, when the culture is devoid of Christ.

ROAD RAGE IN AMERICA

Road rage is anger acted out in negative and even destructive ways while driving. Manifestations of road rage include threats, insults, obscene gestures, tailgating, prolonged honking of the horn, brake checking, swerving toward other drivers, and even shootings. Police receive more than 1,200 reports of road rage incidents every year, many concerning incidents resulting in injuries and even deaths. Road rage incidents have become commonplace in today's God-averse culture as shown by the following facts:[1]

- Over a seven-year period, 12,610 injuries and 218 murders were attributed to road rage in America.
- More than 66 percent of traffic fatalities are caused by aggressive driving.
- In more than 37 percent of aggressive driving incidents at least one of the parties used a firearm.
- The most common manifestations of road rage are prolonged honking of the horn, rude hand gestures, and yelling. However, more than 6 percent of road rage incidents result in physical confrontations between drivers.

What Causes Road Rage?

When surveyed about what causes them to become angry when driving, respondents typically blame the inconsiderate behavior of other drivers.[2] Although this rationale is understandable—no one likes rude drivers— it is still wrong. Claiming someone else is responsible for your anger is just making excuses. No matter how rude other drivers might be, they do not control your temper; you do. This is a truth you can share in love with people who respond in anger to the inconsiderate behavior of other drivers.

People cannot make you mad without your cooperation and permission. Rather than claim other people make you angry, it is more accurate to admit you allow them to make you angry. As fallen people in a fallen world, we all have tempers. At times we lose our tempers and become angry. When this happens, we can choose to control our tempers or let them control us. Losing your temper is a misnomer because failing to control it is a choice.

A biblical truth you can share in love with people who allow themselves to become angry over the inconsiderate behavior of other drivers comes from Proverbs 29:11: "A fool gives full vent to his spirit, but a wise man quietly holds it back." People who quietly hold back their anger might prevent a situation from escalating and eventually getting out of control, even to the point of violence.

Later, when the incident has passed, people often feel better about having acted in a way that prevented a blow-up rather than in a way that contributed to one. Few people will, in retrospect, be happy about allowing a minor incident to get out of control and become a major conflict, especially if things turned violent. After-the-fact regret is common among those who allow themselves to act out their anger in negative ways while driving.

You might also tell people who become angry when driving it is better to be guided by God in these situations than by the behavior of another driver. You might recommend they think about the message in Proverbs 14:17: "A man of quick temper acts foolishly . . ." This message from Scripture means drivers should never allow another person to control their emotions or goad them into doing something they will later regret. As the Bible makes clear, it is our own tempers causing us to act foolishly, not the behavior of other drivers or anyone else.

How Angry Drivers Respond

People who allow themselves to become angry when driving sometimes act out their anger in negative and even destructive ways. Statistics concerning the angry responses of drivers in road rage incidents are shocking. Seven percent of angry drivers get out of their car to verbally confront the other driver, 6 percent throw objects at the other vehicle, 6 percent start a fight with the other driver, 5 percent sideswipe the other vehicle, 5 percent purposely ram the other vehicle, and 5 percent force the other driver off the road.[3] People who allow anger to overrule good sense when driving often try to justify their foolish acts by blaming the other driver for tailgating, driving distractedly, cutting them off, or some other perceived offense.

Nobody enjoys being cut off, tailgated, or inconvenienced by distracted drivers, but hurling insults, throwing objects, starting a fight, ramming another vehicle, or forcing another driver off the road are inappropriate responses no matter what the other driver did. Unfortunately, these are common responses for people who allow themselves

to be guided by their own sense of self-importance rather than the lessons of Holy Scripture. The prevalence of road rage is why it is important for Christians to speak up about this issue and show people a
better way, the way of Christ.

Gender and Age as Factors in Road Rage

Men are more likely to engage in road rage than women. Although
women aged 18–34 do admit to experiencing feelings of road rage, they
are less likely to act on these feelings than men.[4] Because of this, road
rage is primarily, though not exclusively, the domain of men. This is an
important fact to bear in mind for Christians who want to help eliminate this behavior from the culture.

Among men, younger drivers are most often the ones involved in
road-rage incidents. In fact, 14 percent of aggressive driving accidents
involve a driver 18–24 years old.[5] This means individual Christians and
churches can optimize the impact they have in eliminating road rage by
focusing their efforts on young men. Providing wise counsel to young
men might prevent them from doing something rash that could haunt
them the rest of their lives.

Examples of Road-Rage Incidents

Consider this example of a road-rage incident that quickly escalated
and got out of hand, which is often what happens. A big-rig truck was
sitting at a red light. When the light turned green, the truck driver
didn't respond fast enough for the young man in the car behind him.
The young man laid on his horn and made an obscene gesture at the
truck driver. Once the truck was through the light, he pulled off the
road, leaned out of his window, and challenged the young driver to pull
over. When the young man pulled over, the truck driver jumped down
from his cab waving a baseball bat. Seeing this, the young man sped off
just in time.

If this seems like a lot of drama for something as minor as a slow
response to a green light and an obscene gesture, it is. Nevertheless,
road-rage incidents often erupt over minor infractions or inconveniences. In another example, two drivers called the police at the same
time to report each other for road rage. One of the drivers decided to

follow the other one home. When the homeward-bound driver pulled into his driveway, the other driver positioned his car to prevent him from backing out. The driver who was now blocked in his own driveway responded by pulling a gun and firing at the driver who was blocking him. He hit the driver four times, killing him. He also held the now-dead driver's family at gunpoint until police arrived.

A road-rage incident that made international news in 2013 occurred when Alexian Lien found himself caught in the midst of a group of motorcyclists. One of the bikers slammed on his brakes right in front of Lien's car. Lien was unable to stop in time and hit the bike. Angry bikers quickly surrounded Lien's car. Trying to escape, Lien ran over three more bikers. Once the remaining bikers caught up with Lien, they surrounded his car, smashed out his window, pulled him through a window, and beat him unconscious while his family watched from inside the car.[6] All of this was caught on camera and replayed on national television. It turned out one of the bikers involved in the beating was an off-duty police officer.

In another incident, when a driver forced him out of his lane, Alan Garcia threw up his hands in frustration. Seeing this reaction, the driver of the offending car—Tony Torres—began chasing Garcia's car on Interstate 40 in New Mexico. When he caught up with Garcia, Torres pulled out a gun and started firing. He missed Garcia, but one of his rounds hit and killed Garcia's four-year old daughter. For something as minor and inoffensive as another driver throwing up his hands, Torres was willing to shoot and kill a four-year old child.[7]

In yet another incident, a grandmother was driving with her newborn granddaughter in a car seat. Because she was carrying precious cargo, the grandmother was driving slowly and being extra cautious. Her slow rate of speed angered the driver behind her who sped up, switched lanes to come abreast of the grandmother's car, and fired into it with a handgun. The angry driver missed the grandmother but killed the baby. The perpetrator was willing to kill an innocent little baby because her grandmother was driving too slowly to suit him.

Road-rage incidents such as these are shocking, but not uncommon. In a culture devoid of Christ, human life has no value. In a culture where human life has no value, there are going to be people willing to kill innocent children just because they were inconvenienced or did not like the reaction of another driver. Road-rage is just one more of the tragic consequences associated with this kind of culture.

Almost as disturbing as these sinful acts is the fascination there seems to be with them. How many hours of video of this kind of thing have been posted and watched?

SIDELINE RAGE IN AMERICA

A close cousin of road rage is *sideline rage.* Sideline rage is anger acted out in negative and even violent ways by spectators at sports events. More often than not the event in question is a youth sports game in baseball, football, soccer, volleyball, hockey, or basketball. Angry spectators, often parents of the children playing, verbally berate game officials, coaches, and other players, occasionally even attacking them physically.

While parents of past generations taught their children the value of good sportsmanship, many parents today teach their children just the opposite by setting a bad example. Children in their formative years learn from the examples set by their parents and other adults.

Some parents have become so vicariously competitive and determined to see their children win they erupt when things are not going their way. Their attacks are usually verbal, but increasingly they are physical. Coaches, game officials, and even children on the opposing team have been physically attacked by parents who lose their tempers, including mothers. Here are just a few examples of what irate parents, coaches, and other adults have done at youth sports events:[8]

- A father from Reading, Massachusetts was watching his son's hockey practice when he got into a dispute with another father. He became irate and beat the other father to death by continually banging his head against the concrete floor.
- An angry soccer coach who disputed a call head-butted the referee breaking his nose.
- A fight broke out at a football game in El Paso, Texas involving more than thirty adults, most of them parents. During the melee, one father stabbed another between the eyes.
- A father who was angry because his son wasn't selected for the all-star team knocked the team's coach down and kicked him.

- A volleyball coach was fired from his job for bringing a meat cleaver to school after having an argument with a referee.
- A thirty-six-year-old coach choked a fifteen-year-old umpire who was calling a tee-ball game for children aged five and six.
- A parent poisoned the players on the opposing youth football team to ensure her son's team would win the championship.
- A dentist sharpened the faceguard on his son's football helmet so the boy could slash opposing players. Five players and the referee were injured.
- A parent paid a ten-year-old pitcher two dollars to purposely hit an opposing batter in a Little League game.

As with road rage, parents who engage in sideline rage tend to justify their actions by blaming their behavior on someone or something else. The kinds of excuses parents give for becoming irate at their children's sports events include "the referee made a bad call," "the coach took my son out of the game," "the opposing coach is cheating," and "the umpire called my daughter out when she was clearly safe." What is shocking is parents would consider these kinds of things, even if true, valid reasons for verbally and even physically attacking coaches, game officials, other parents, or opposing players.

How Sideline Rage Affects Children

Children who play on youth sports teams are in their formative years. They learn and develop by watching their parents and other adults. What they are learning by observing sideline rage at youth sports events is not good. This is a message you may want to share in love with adults you know who become irate at youth sports events and inappropriately act out their anger rather than controlling it.

Children in their formative years are like sponges. They soak up what they see and hear adults doing. Further, they learn more from examples than from words. For parents who engage in sideline rage to tell their children, "Do as I say not as I do" is a waste of time. Invariably children will do what their parents and other adults do. This is precisely what is happening with children who play youth sports.

Consider how children in their formative years think. If it is acceptable for parents and other adults to yell obscenities at opposing coaches, players, parents, and game officials, it must be acceptable for children to do the same. If it is okay for parents and other adults to physically attack opposing coaches, players, parents, and game officials, it must be okay for children to do the same thing. The influence adult examples have on the development and attitudes of children cannot be overstated.

Rather than teaching young people by example that anger and violence are acceptable responses to differences of opinion, parents should be teaching them biblical exhortations such as the one in Ephesians 4:31: "Let all bitterness and wrath and anger and clamor and slander be put away from you, along with all malice." Rather than teaching young people anger acted out in negative and destructive ways is acceptable, parents should be teaching them about the fruit of the Spirit as set forth in Galatians 5:22: "But the fruit of the spirit is love, joy, peace, patience, kindness, goodness, faithfulness . . ."

Here is some wise counsel you can share in love with parents who engage in sideline rage:

- Their example is teaching children violent, destructive behavior is acceptable. Jails and prisons are full of people who think violence and destructive behavior are acceptable ways to respond to differences.
- People who learn to treat others as children of God created in His image and deserving of the respect, patience, and grace this entails will go much farther in life than those who become disagreeable or even violent every time there is a point of contention. People who learn to control their tempers and disagree without being disagreeable have integrity and better character than those who let their anger control them and, as a result, act out in destructive ways.

WHAT YOU CAN DO ABOUT ROAD RAGE AND SIDELINE RAGE

To play a positive role in reducing road rage and sideline rage, begin by studying what the Bible has to say about these topics. Helpful verses for providing wise counsel to people who let their anger control their actions include the following:

- **James 1:19–20:** *"Know this, my beloved brothers: let every person be quick to hear, slow to speak, slow to anger; for the anger of man does not produce the righteousness of God."* These verses may help you provide wise counsel to people who let their tempers get the better of them and act unwisely as a result. Both verses can be especially effective if the person you are trying to help is a Christian but both can also be used to point unbelievers to Christ.
- **Proverbs 14:29:** *"Whoever is slow to anger has great understanding, but he who has a hasty temper exalts folly."* This verse may help you make the point that nothing good comes out of letting one's temper get out of control. The message this verse conveys is do not let your temper cause you to do something you will regret later. Rash actions, once taken, cannot be taken back.
- **Ephesians 4:32:** *"Be kind to one another, tenderhearted, forgiving one another, as God in Christ forgave you."* Even unbelievers understand they need forgiveness from time to time. This verse may help you show how forgiven people must be willing to forgive others and overlooking what you think is a bad call qualifies as forgiveness. This verse may also help you point people who succumb to anger to Christ.
- **Proverbs 19:11:** *"Good sense makes one slow to anger, and it is his glory to overlook an offense."* This verse may help you demonstrate there will always be situations that make us angry if we let them, but rather than give into anger it is better to overlook offenses both supposed and real. Overlooking things that otherwise might make us angry will bring better results in the long run than losing our temper. You might also point out how overlooking something stirring anger in you is wiser than responding in a way you will later regret.

To speak the truth in love about road rage and sideline rage as part of the wise counsel you give others, you must first know the truth, and God's Word is the truth. Knowing what the Bible says about anger will equip you to point the way to Christ for people who let their tempers get the better of them. The previous verses recommended are just to get you started. The Bible has much more to say about the issue of anger and, by association, road rage and sideline rage.

Once you have studied what Scripture teaches about anger, pray God will enter the hearts of people who succumb to rage and replace their out-of-control emotions with the love and patience of Christ. If you are not sure how to pray about this issue, recite the following prayer:

> *Lord, I am concerned about (Robert). He often lets his temper get the better of him. When he does this, (Robert) loses control and acts rashly. I am afraid he is going to do something destructive or violent, something he will regret. Lord, (Robert) allows even the smallest inconveniences to trigger his temper. I pray You intercede in his life and replace the anger always just below the surface in (Robert) with the love, patience, caring, and forgiveness of Christ. I pray You turn him from a path that will eventually lead (Robert) to a bad place. I ask these things in the name of Jesus. Amen.*

When you have prayed for the individual you are concerned about, the next step is to make sure your children and grandchildren learn to control their tempers. Teach them to exemplify the fruit of the Spirit in their lives. Above all, remember the best way to teach these things to your children and grandchildren is by example. Children in their formative years will be influenced more by your example than your words. Words are still important, but make sure your example reinforces your words.

Having studied the Bible, prayed, and taught your own children and grandchildren to treat others with respect, patience, and grace, encourage your church to provide learning opportunities for the congregation and community teaching the following: [9]

- Winning is good but it is not everything. Playing hard and doing your best while maintaining godly character is more important. Those who play hard and do their best while maintaining godly character will win their share of games, but they will also win something even more important. They will win the approval of their Lord and Savior.

- Remember, your sport is a game not a war, and the other team is your opponent not your enemy.
- No matter what happens in a game, if you feel compelled to say something, make sure it is positive, helpful, and encouraging. Others are watching and they might just follow your example.
- Let the game officials call the game without comments or other negative reactions. Those who are not in the arena should not criticize those who are.
- Never let the bad behavior of opposing coaches or players influence your behavior. Behave in all situations as if Christ is standing beside you watching—because He is in the presence of the Holy Spirit.

Anger-induced phenomena such as road rage and sideline rage are less likely to occur in a culture centered on Christ. Be prepared to make this point when you speak the truth in love to people who engage in these despicable practices. Further, when you talk with unbelievers who are disturbed by the bad behavior they observe at sports contests, let them know they cannot have it both ways. When a society pushes Christ out, it lets Satan in. Road rage and sideline rage are tools of Satan. People cannot continue to reject God, accept sin, and expect there to be no consequences. Road rage and sideline rage are just two more examples of what happens in a nation rejecting God and accepting sin.

CHAPTER 13

DEMISE OF THE TRADITIONAL FAMILY

But if anyone does not provide for his relatives, and especially
for members of his household, he has denied the faith and is
worse than an unbeliever.

—1 Timothy 5:8

The traditional family, going all the way back to the first book of the Bible, Genesis, has been defined as one with two parents in the household: a father and a mother. An extended traditional family includes grandparents, great-grandparents, aunts, uncles, nieces, nephews, and cousins. These are the "relatives" mentioned in 1 Timothy 5:8. The message in this verse from Scripture makes it clear family is important to God. Unfortunately, because Christ is being removed from the culture in America, the traditional family continues to decline right before our eyes.

Traditional families are based on the sustained marriages of men and women. This is why when a man and a woman are joined in marriage in a Bible-believing church their vows include words to the effect they will remain married forever through good times and bad, in sickness and in health. A marriage blessed by God is one intended to last until the spouses are parted by death. This fact is why the findings of a study undertaken by the Joint Economic Committee of Congress in 2020 are so disturbing. Titled "The Demise of the Happy Two-Parent Home," the findings of this Congressional study are shocking:[1]

- In 1962, 71 percent of women aged fifteen to forty-four were married. By 2019 this number declined to just 42 percent.
- In the 1960s, less than 1 percent of couples living together were unmarried. Today that number has risen to more than 12 percent.
- In 1960, births to unmarried women represented just 5 percent of all births. By 2018 this number rose to 40 percent. This number would be even higher were it not for the prevalence of abortion.
- In 1970, 85 percent of children in America lived with two parents. By 2019, this number fell to 70 percent.

What these statistics demonstrate is the traditional family, as defined in the Bible, is fading away. Christians need to know why the traditional family is in peril and why rescuing it is important.

WHY IS THE TRADITIONAL AMERICAN FAMILY IN PERIL?

The overriding reason behind the demise of the traditional family in America is the systematic rejection of God and acceptance of sin pushing Christ and His Word out of the culture. The biblical model concerning family structure is of no interest to people who look to themselves rather than God's Word for guidance in life. Hence, the rejection of God coupled with the acceptance of sin is the root cause of the demise of the traditional family. There is also an important contributing cause.

The study conducted by the Joint Economic Committee of Congress listed the growth of the welfare state as a major factor in the demise of the traditional two-parent family.[2] Welfare was originally envisioned as a temporary safety net, but continual increases in the monetary and material benefits it provides have turned the safety net into a comfortable hammock and welfare into a way of life. Welfare now provides a level of support enabling and even encouraging single mothers to stay single and on welfare permanently. Women who collect welfare risk losing their eligibility if they get married. Because of this, welfare is no longer viewed as a temporary expedient by many recipients. Instead, it has become a way of life and even legacy.

Consider this finding from the Joint Economic Committee of Congress: the financial and material benefits of welfare for single mothers are 133 percent higher today than they were in 1940 and 56 percent higher than they were in 1960.[3] When the government requires remaining single as a condition for collecting welfare, no one should be surprised when women do not get married. When the government incentivizes remaining on welfare rather than going to work, nobody should be surprised when recipients refuse to work. This point crystallized during the COVID debacle when the government shut down businesses and paid people to stay home. As of this writing, the workforce is still gravely depleted.

Another factor undermining the traditional family is the concept of same-sex marriage. The growing number of same-sex marriages has created a new "family" structure in which both parents are either male or female. Adoption of children by same-sex couples is on the rise. Further, the concept of same-sex parenting is rapidly gaining broad-based acceptance as elementary school children are required to read books with titles such as *Timmy Has Two Mommies* or *Susie Has Two Daddies*. Many schools also teach young children to avoid using masculine or feminine pronouns.

WHY IS THE DEMISE OF THE TRADITIONAL AMERICAN FAMILY IMPORTANT?

Since our country was established, the most important institution in America has been the family, not the presidency, Congress, the Supreme Court, public education, business, industry, the military, or higher education. It has been the family. No institution has historically done more to develop, support, and encourage young people than the family. Children in stable, traditional two-parent families enjoy numerous socioeconomic advantages over children in single-parent households, particularly when those families are connected to a church. Consider just a few advantages of the traditional family. Children raised in stable, traditional two-parent households . . .[4]

- are less likely to experience academic, social, emotional, or cognitive problems; benefits that stay with them into adulthood;
- typically have greater access to economic and community resources because their parents are able to pool their time, money, and energy;
- receive more of their parents' attention because the parents are less distracted by the everyday challenges of just making ends meet. With fewer distractions, the parents can be more involved in the lives of their children and more invested in their success;
- are more likely to graduate from high school and college;
- have higher employment rates and lower out-of-wedlock birth rates than their counterparts in single-parent families;
- tend to be healthier than those from single-parent households. For example, following a divorce, children are 50 percent more likely to develop health problems than their counterparts in stable, traditional two-parent households;
- enjoy higher levels of academic achievement and are less likely to exhibit problem behaviors than their counterparts in single-parent families;
- are 82 percent less likely to live in poverty than children in single-parent households.

What these facts about the traditional biblically-defined family say is two parents working together as a team in accordance with God's Word can provide a stable, enriching, beneficial environment for children. Matthew 19:19 admonishes young people to "Honor your father and mother," and, "You shall love your neighbor as yourself." Children who grow up in traditional two-parent families are more likely to learn this lesson, a lesson that will serve them well in life.

The benefits of growing up in a traditional two-parent family are why the on-going demise of this institution is of concern; it is the most important institution in America when it comes to ensuring the brightest possible future for our country. Coupled, the family and the church make a powerfully effective team when it comes to developing young people. You have probably heard it said many times, "children are our future." This being the case, the importance of reversing the present course and restoring the traditional American family cannot be overstated.

THE TRAGEDY OF DIVORCE IN AMERICA

One of the most devastating factors in the demise of the traditional family is divorce. America has one of the highest divorce rates in the world. Consider the following 2020 statistics about divorce in our country:[5]

- The current divorce rate in America is double what it was in 1960.
- Approximately 41 percent of first marriages end in divorce.
- Approximately 60 percent of second marriages end in divorce.
- Approximately 73 percent of third marriages end in divorce.
- There is a divorce in America every thirteen seconds or 277 divorces per hour, 6,646 per day, 46,523 per week, and 2,419,196 per year.
- Women file for divorce more often than men (66 percent of divorce proceedings are initiated by women).
- During the average wedding reception, 1,385 divorces occur.

The current divorce rate of 16.9 percent per 1,000 married women is actually down from the all-time high of 22.6 percent in the early 1980s.[6] However, this fact is deceiving. The divorce rate is lower than the all-time high in large measure because young people are putting off marriage longer and more are simply choosing to cohabitate without the benefit of marriage, not because couples are less likely to divorce. Further, divorce statistics do not include the broken relationships of unmarried but cohabitating couples.

Why People Divorce in America

Divorced people blame the break-up of their marriages on a variety of factors, most of which miss an important point. With Christ at the center of a marriage, the following reasons are less likely to occur in the first place, but without Christ they are more likely to occur. Factors often leading to divorce include:[7]

- Lack of commitment
- Argue too much

- Infidelity
- Married too young
- Unrealistic expectations
- Lack of equality in the relationship
- Lack of preparation for marriage
- Domestic violence

Marriages centered on Christ are not problem-free, and no one should expect them to be. All relationships have their ups and downs. However, a major difference between a Christ-centered marriage and a me-centered marriage is a commitment to Christ gives couples an avenue for working through their problems in a loving and caring way. This is a truth you can speak in love to people whose marriages are falling apart.

Ice-Cream Love Compared with Christian Love in Marriages

Christ-centered marriages are based on 1 Corinthians 13. This is the defining verse in Scripture when it comes to Christian love. It makes the point that love is a verb, not just an emotion or a feeling. The world talks about "falling in love" and "falling out of love." Love you can fall into or out of is not Christian love. It is better described as *ice-cream love.*

People claim to "love" ice cream, but they don't. Rather, they love what ice cream does for them: the way it looks, tastes, and makes them feel. They love the way it satisfies their urge for something sweet, creamy, and cold. Ice-cream love is based on selfishness, and selfishness is a marriage killer. The kind of love that sustains a marriage is selfless.

What the world calls love is better referred to as infatuation. Infatuation is a feeling of intense amorous interest that is often temporary. This is why there are so many couples who once promised to love and cherish each other until "death do we part" who, though still alive, are now divorced. They were temporarily infatuated with each other, but they were not in love. Christian love as described in 1 Corinthians 13 is not something you fall into or out of. It is something you do. The kind of love God expects of us is a verb. Further, Christian love is about "you" not "me." When you love someone, your chief concern is for their best interests, not what they can do for you or how they make you feel.

Love is demonstrated by doing certain things prescribed in Scripture and not doing other "proscribed" things. First Corinthians 13:4–6 describes biblical love in the following terms:

- Love is patient
- Love is kind
- Love is not envious
- Love is not boastful
- Love is not arrogant
- Love is not rude
- Love does not insist on getting its own way
- Love is not irritable
- Love is not resentful
- Love does not enjoy indulging in wrongdoing
- Love is truthful

Marriages based on these eleven factors set forth in 1 Corinthians 13 are not likely to end up in divorce. A Christ-filled life is the best guarantee of a sustained marriage. An individual with strong religious beliefs, particularly Christian beliefs, is 14 percent less likely to divorce than someone lacking those beliefs.[8] As you talk with people who are struggling in their marriages, be prepared to share the biblical definition of love from 1 Corinthians 13 with them. Approaching the relationship from the perspective of selflessness rather than selfishness can save and sustain a marriage.

WHAT YOU CAN DO ABOUT THE DEMISE OF THE TRADITIONAL FAMILY

To play a positive role in helping revive the traditional family, begin by studying what the Bible has to say about marriage and family. Helpful verses for providing wise counsel to people who are considering marriage or who are struggling in their marriages include the following:

- **Genesis 2:24:** *"Therefore a man shall leave his father and his mother and hold fast to his wife, and they shall become one flesh."* This verse may help you make the important point that God ordains marriage, not cohabitation and not single-parent families.

- **Hebrews 13:4:** *"Let marriage be held in honor among all, and let the marriage bed be undefiled, for God will judge the sexually immoral and adulterous."* This verse may help when you need to have a difficult conversation with a person who is being unfaithful in marriage. It shows how God knows what is happening, is not pleased by infidelity, and will judge those involved in adultery.
- **Ephesians 5:33:** *"However, let each of you love his wife as himself, and let the wife see that she respects her husband."* This verse may be helpful if you are trying to provide wise counsel to spouses who are failing to love and respect each other. Husbands who enter marriage for self-serving reasons may not understand what it means to love their wives. Wives who enter marriage for the wrong reasons may not understand what it means to respect their husbands. This verse makes the point that love and respect are essential in marriage.
- **Malachi 2:16:** *"For the man who does not love his wife but divorces her, says the LORD, the God of Israel, covers his garment with violence, says the LORD of hosts. So guard yourselves in your spirit, and do not be faithless."* This verse may help you provide wise counsel to someone who is contemplating divorce. Clearly, the Lord disapproves of divorce except under very specifically defined circumstances. This verse warns against casually tossing aside a marriage.

To speak the truth in love about marriage and family as part of wise counsel you provide others, you must know the truth, and God's Word is the truth. Knowing what the Bible says about marriage and family will equip you to point the way to Christ for people who are contemplating marriage as well as married couples who are struggling and considering divorce. The verses recommended here are just to get you started. The Bible has much more to say about the subjects of marriage and family.

Once you have studied what Scripture says about marriage and family, pray God will intercede in marriages that are falling apart and help the spouses rebuild their marriages on a solid biblical foundation. Pray God will help couples replace the infatuation of ice-cream love with biblical love as defined in 1 Corinthians 13. If you are not sure how to pray about this issue, recite the following prayer:

> *Lord, I am concerned about (John and Kathy). Their marriage is in trouble. (John and Kathy) married on the basis of infatuation rather than biblical love. They both have a self-serving attitude toward marriage. I pray You intercede in this marriage and help this couple rebuild their relationship on a foundation of biblical love. Take away their selfishness and replace it with selflessness. Help each of these young people put the best interests of the other ahead of their own self-centered desires. Lord, I ask these things in the holy name of Jesus. Amen.*

When you have prayed for the people you are concerned about, the next step is to ensure your children and grandchildren learn about biblical love and its place in marriage. It is important to share what Scripture teaches about marriage with your children and grandchildren. It is also important to demonstrate by example what Scripture teaches. One of the best ways to prepare your children and grandchildren for marriage is to show them what a godly marriage looks like. If we raise our children well, we can make substantial headway in restoring the traditional family in just one generation.

Having studied the Bible, prayed, and taught your own children and grandchildren about the sanctity of marriage, consider trying the following additional strategies. They may help you play a positive role in restoring the traditional family:

- Be prepared to speak the truth in love to people who are contemplating marriage. Explain the difference between ice-cream love and biblical love.
- Be prepared to show people who are struggling in their marriage the difference 1 Corinthians 13 can make in overcoming the various reasons people give for divorcing.
- Know the biblical reasons in Matthew 19:9 and 1 Corinthians 7:10–16 for pursuing a divorce and be prepared to share them with people who are contemplating a divorce. Note that these verses state

the instances in which divorce is allowable, not mandatory. If the offending spouse is repentant and willing to atone for his or her sins, reconciliation may be possible. However, if there is physical, verbal, or emotional abuse, the church should help the victimized spouse seek safety from the abuser.

- Encourage your pastor and church to provide premarital counseling for members of the congregation and community. Young people who are fully aware of what the Bible teaches about marriage and who take these teachings to heart before marrying are less likely to divorce.

- Encourage your pastor and church to provide marriage counseling for couples who are struggling in their marriages. There are few problems in a marriage that cannot be overcome if the spouses commit to the teaching in 1 Corinthians 13 about biblical love being a verb.

- Encourage your church to offer marriage seminars open to the community teaching participants about the value of the traditional family, the definition of a Christ-centered marriage, and biblical love as explained in 1 Corinthians 13.

The traditional, biblically-defined family is the most important institution in America, but it can survive and thrive only in a Christ-centered culture. Be prepared to make this point to people who are contemplating marriage on the basis of ice-cream love or who plan to cohabitate rather than get married. When you talk with unbelievers who are concerned about the demise of the traditional family, let them know they cannot have it both ways. They cannot continue to reject God, accept sin, and expect there to be no consequences. Broken relationships, divorces, and destroyed families are examples of what happens in a nation that rejects God but accepts sin.

CHAPTER 14

GUTTER POLITICS

"Tell us, then, what you think. Is it lawful to pay taxes to Caesar, or not?" But Jesus, aware of their malice said, "Why put me to the test, you hypocrites? Show me the coin for the tax." And they brought him a denarius. And Jesus said to them, "Whose likeness and inscription is this?" They said, "Caesar's." Then he said to them, "Therefore render to Caesar the things that are Caesar's, and to God the things that are God's."

—Matthew 22:17–21

Self-interest is the heart and soul of politics. Because the political process is driven by self-interest, it is a contact sport. Politics can be messy, frustrating, and sometimes ugly. This has always been the case, but in recent years things have gotten worse. How politicians, particularly those on the left, approach the process has changed, and not for the better. National politics in America has gone from being a contact sport to being a gutter sport.

The goal of politicians has long been to gain and retain power. Traditionally, this was done by convincing the voting public of the superiority of one's principles and policies. The American electorate has a history of favoring policies that serve the long-term interests of our country rather than those serving the interests of an individual politician or political party. Because of this expectation, even in times of political discord, there has been room for collaboration and cooperation between the two major political parties.

Unfortunately, as America's culture has plunged into darkness, so has the political process. Statesmanship and cooperation for the good of the country have been replaced by a new approach aptly called *gutter politics*. The ultimate goal of politicians has not changed; it is still to gain and retain power. The difference is gutter politicians are willing to do anything, no matter how underhanded, inappropriate, or unethical, to achieve this goal. Rather than trying to convince the voting public of the efficacy of their principles and policies, gutter politicians engage in the politics of personal destruction and character assassination to demonize their opponents.

Rather than offer superior policies to voters, gutter politicians attempt to destroy the opposition. Rather than question the validity of their opponent's policies, gutter politicians question their character. False accusations, derogatory labels, snide insinuations, and suggestive innuendo are all tactics used by gutter politicians to demonize opponents. Two goals of gutter politicians are to destroy political opponents by assassinating their character and to ward off future opponents by making the personal cost of running for office too high.

The weaker the positions of gutter politicians, the stronger their attacks on opponents. The less valid their policies, the more vigorous their attacks. The more valid their opponent's positions, the shriller the false accusations of gutter politicians become. Politicians who operate in the gutter do so because they have nothing of substance to offer the American public. They would do well to heed the message in Titus 3:9: "But avoid foolish controversies, genealogies, dissensions, and quarrels about the law, for they are unprofitable and worthless." "Unprofitable" and "worthless" are apt descriptions of the tactics of gutter politicians.

The government established by our Founders envisioned elected officials who would base their policies and decisions on what is best for the nation rather than their own personal interests. The concept is known as *statesmanship*. These citizen legislators would serve for a period of time and then voluntarily step aside as did America's first president, George Washington. They were not career politicians.

Our Founders would be shocked to learn there are career politicians whose sole aim is to gain power and retain it forever, remaining in office for the whole of their working lives. They would be even more shocked to learn career politicians often become wealthy during their time in office. Most of the Founders sacrificed personally and financially to serve our country. Nine sacrificed their lives and seventeen lost their fortunes and property. Our Founders opposed lifelong office holding because they knew career politicians would contaminate the political process. This is precisely what the gutter politicians of today are doing.

POLITICS OF PERSONAL DESTRUCTION: A CLOSER LOOK

As has already been established, the *politics of personal destruction* is a strategy for seeking to gain and retain political power by undermining, demonizing, and destroying the opposition. Those who engage in this despicable practice are aided and abetted by the mainstream media. Practitioners of the politics of personal destruction are fond of using a tactic attributed to Adolph Hitler's propaganda minister, Joseph Goebbels.

Goebbels believed all that was necessary for lies to be accepted as truth was for them to be repeated loudly enough and often enough. His demented strategy gave rise to the adage: *A lie repeated often enough becomes the truth.* But this adage is itself a lie; the Word of God is the only source of truth. All truths spring from His Word. Anything not comporting with the Word of God is a lie no matter how loudly or often it is repeated. Tragically but not surprisingly Hitler's use of Goebbels's tactic eventually led to the complete destruction of his country as well as the suicides of he and Goebbels.

Eventual destruction is the likely outcome for political movements based on lies, distortion, and deception, a fact you may have to share in love with advocates of the politics of personal destruction. If you have an opportunity to engage in dialogue with a gutter politician or someone who supports one, Philippians 4:8 may be helpful: "Finally, brothers, whatever is true, whatever is honorable, whatever is just, whatever is pure, whatever is lovely, whatever is commendable, if there is an excellence, if there is anything worthy of praise, think about these things." The politics of personal destruction will eventually destroy not just its victims but its practitioners.

Because the German people believed Hitler's often repeated lies, their country, their homes, and their lives were utterly destroyed in an unnecessary and unjust war. Millions died, including Hitler and his minions, in a senseless and brutal waste of lives that could have been avoided had German citizens looked to the Word of God for the truth rather than a corrupt gutter politician who based his vision for their country on lies. One can only wonder if the conflagration in Europe known as World War II would have even happened had the German people heeded the message in Psalm 120:2: "Deliver me, O LORD, from lying lips, from a deceitful tongue."

Supported by the mainstream media, gutter politicians use Goebbels's principle as one of their favorite tactics. Unfortunately, a lot of people are gullible enough to believe what they hear and read in the media and on social media without questioning its validity. Thinking people know better. Biased, ill-informed, or agenda-driven reporting is easy to recognize if people will take the time to think about what they hear and read. Unfortunately, there are a lot of people who do not take the time to be discerning. This fact presents Christians with a challenge. A message you may have to share with people who naively accept and believe what they hear on the news or read on social media comes from Matthew 7:15: "Beware of false prophets, who come to you in sheep's clothing but inwardly are ravenous wolves."

A message you may need to share with family members, friends, and colleagues who form their opinions based on social media posts and mainstream media reporting is the one in Proverbs 14:5: "A faithful witness does not lie, but a false witness breathes out lies." You may have to explain how mainstream media reporters and social media posters are often false witnesses because they are trying to advance an agenda based on something other than the truth. Anything reported in the media or posted on social media not comporting with Holy Scripture is false, regardless the source. Truth is non-negotiable. It has one source and that source—Holy Scripture—defines it.

People who engage in the politics of personal destruction have two goals. First, they hope their underhanded tactic will eliminate candidates or judicial nominees they don't want elected to office or appointed to the bench. Second, they hope to frighten away future candidates by demonstrating what they will be put through should they seek elective or appointed office. The message of gutter politicians who use this shady tactic is simple: if you choose to run for office or seek an appointed position, we will destroy you.

Supreme Court Justices Clarence Thomas and Brett Kavanaugh are examples of individuals who were subjected to the politics of personal destruction at its worst. Gutter politicians turned their confirmation hearings into sordid soap operas. To secure their seats on the Supreme Court, these two honorable, capable men had to endure unrelenting libel, slander, accusations, attacks, innuendo, and bullying.

They were vilified, disparaged, and denigrated on national television for the world—including their families, friends, and colleagues—to see. In spite of the abuse both men were subjected to, Justices Thomas and Kavanaugh courageously persevered and were eventually confirmed by the Senate to serve on the Supreme Court. However, the price they paid for the privilege of serving their country was high and the personal trauma they were forced to endure was unconscionable.

One of the most blatant examples of the politics of personal destruction was the war waged against Donald Trump during his campaign, through his time in the Oval Office, and continues as of this writing. The personal attacks on Trump did not stop even after it was shown they had no basis in fact. President Trump was subjected to not just one but two baseless, biased, politically motivated impeachments in attempts to destroy him and any future aspirations he might have in politics. Both impeachment efforts came to nothing when the Senate refused to go along with the gutter politics of House Democrats.

The second impeachment occurred after Trump was out of office and no longer president. The goal of the gutter politicians who led this unconstitutional effort was to destroy Trump and any aspirations he might have of running for president in the future. The treatment of Donald Trump by gutter politicians before he was elected, during his term of office, and after he left is an example of the politics of personal destruction at its worst. The anti-Trump movement was based on the worst of political motives: hatred. Perhaps the most telling and what may have the most impact going forward is the number of so-called Conservative Republicans who piled onto the destroy-Trump train.

CHARACTER ASSASSINATION: A CLOSER LOOK

A favorite tactic of gutter politicians who engage in the politics of personal destruction is *character assassination.* Character assassination involves using false accusations, distorted information, suggestive innuendo, deliberate half-truths, blatant exaggerations, spurious rumors, snide insinuations, and ad hominem attacks to undermine the reputation and credibility of political opponents. With this tactic, gutter politicians attempt to portray opponents not just as unworthy of holding public office but as a bad people.

For textbook examples of character assassination let us return to the cases of Supreme Court nominees Clarence Thomas and Brett Kavanaugh as well as President Donald Trump. These cases were glaring examples of gutter politicians engaging in character assassination, examples a lot of people at all points on the political spectrum found disturbing. Only political malcontents blinded by hatred and guided by a self-serving agenda would stoop to the moral lows displayed by gutter politicians in these three cases. The attacks on Judge Kavanaugh illustrate the methods employed by gutter politicians.

The Senate hearings for Brett Kavanaugh prior to his confirmation as a Supreme Court justice gave the world a close-up look at character assassination and how it is used by gutter politicians. When nominated by President Donald Trump, Kavanaugh was a highly-qualified judge with a distinguished record and impeccable credentials, an ideal candidate to serve on the Supreme Court. However, afraid he would vote to overturn *Roe v. Wade* if confirmed, gutter politicians used every dirty trick in their playbook of corrupt practices to derail his nomination.

Their ad hominem attacks on Judge Kavanaugh included false accusations, unfounded rumors, media manipulation, distortion of information, defamation, misdirection, half-truths, innuendo, and insinuation, all intended to portray him as a bad person unworthy of a seat on the Court. It wasn't enough for leftist senators to oppose Kavanaugh's confirmation; they wanted to destroy him. Their tactic of choice was character assassination.

Brett Kavanaugh's Senate confirmation hearings pulled back the curtain to give the world a peek at how gutter politicians use character assassination for their self-serving purposes. Such a public display of manufactured vitriol, blatant hypocrisy, and venomous hatred had not been witnessed by the American public since the Clarence Thomas confirmation hearings in 1991.

The character assassination of Judge Kavanaugh left an indelible stain on the body politic in America, undermining further the public's respect for and trust in Congress. This is saying a lot since Congress perennially ranks as one of the least respected, least trusted institutions in America. Many Americans who watched the Kavanaugh hearings on television thought gutter politicians stooped as low as they possibly could go. They were wrong.

Even before he was elected president, Donald Trump became the target of gutter politicians driven not just by a thirst for power but by a mindless hatred unsurpassed in American politics. Had Trump served 200 years earlier, duels would have been fought over the accusations made against him. For all four years of his administration, President Trump was subjected to an unrelenting cascade of false accusations, unfounded innuendo, and venomous diatribes. The impeachment sham after Trump left office was not only groundless, it was un-Constitutional; a fact ignored by gutter politicians determined to destroy Trump and repel anyone who might want to follow in the trail he blazed.

The attempts at character assassination aimed at Clarence Thomas, Brett Kavanaugh, and Donald Trump left a lot of Americans wondering why there is so much divisiveness and so little cooperation in national politics these days. They want to know why politicians, particularly those in Congress, put so much effort into destroying political opponents rather than doing the job they were elected to do. In short, they want to know why politicians who are elected to serve in a government of the people, by the people, and for the people spend so little time serving the people.

This is a question you may have to help fellow Americans of all political persuasions answer. The answer is simple but profound. Cooperation and collaboration are missing in American politics because our country is being pulled away from its moral foundation, core values, and Christian principles by activists and organizations actively rejecting God and embracing sin. Because of their efforts to remove God from every-day life in America, anti-God ideologues have turned our country into the house divided warned of in Mark 3:24. America has become a house that will not stand unless we do what is necessary to reclaim the culture for Christ. American culture has already devolved to the point America no longer resembles the nation created by our Founders.

GUTTER POLITICIANS UNDERMINE AMERICA'S MORAL FOUNDATION

By and large, America's Founders were committed Christians. More than half of the men who signed the Declaration of Independence held seminary degrees. Meetings of the Continental Congress were opened and closed with prayer. In their research, our Founders consulted and cited the Bible more than any other source. Because they were well-versed in the teachings of Scripture, the Founders knew the democratic form of government they established had an Achilles Heel: it would work only as long as it rested on a strong moral foundation.

Reject God and you destroy America's moral foundation. Destroy America's moral foundation and you open the door to gutter politics and every form of corruption. Gutter politicians serve themselves rather than the citizens who elected them; they put personal interest ahead of national interest. Their own supposed best interests, no matter how misguided, are their only compass. They have no moral compass. This sad situation should sound familiar to anyone who monitors the political process in America.

Gutter politicians do not just ignore the moral foundation estab-lished by our Founders, they reject it. Anything they have to do to retain power is acceptable, no matter how bad it is for our country. To gutter politicians, the ends justify the means no matter how immoral, uneth-ical, or destructive. Gutter politics is narcissistic self-interest at its worst and it violates the basic tenets of our Declaration of Independence, Constitution, and founding vision.

Without moral restraint, a win-by-any-means approach to politics is perfectly acceptable provided, of course, you are the winner. The rea-son gutter politicians are drawn to the politics of personal destruction and character assassination is they reject the moral foundation and core values that made America both good and great. They have no compunction against tearing down what America's Founders built provided doing so suits their self-interests, even if only in the short run. For gutter politicians, today is all that matters; tomorrow is someone else's problem.

Gutter politicians want what they want, when they want it, and how they want it. They rarely consider the long-term consequences of their actions. They tend toward instant gratification without a thought to what might result down the road. In fact, when their actions inevitably meet with negative results and lead to public disapproval, gutter politicians simply shift the blame to others. They are masters at finger pointing and blame shifting, but steadfastly refuse to accept responsibility for the consequences of their actions.

The best-known line from President Abraham Lincoln's Gettysburg Address was his description of the government of the United States as a "government of the people, by the people, and for the people." With these memorable words, Lincoln paid tribute to America's form of self-government by a Constitutional Republic. However, with apologies to our 16th President, a government "of the people, by the people, and for the people" is a government of sinners, by sinners, and for sinners.

This fact is why the moral guidance provided by God's Word is so important in any government. In Lincoln's defense, he understood the necessity of moral restraints in government, but served as president at a time when it was unnecessary to state the obvious. The need for moral restraints in government, during Lincoln's lifetime, could be taken for granted as a widely accepted truth among his fellow Americans. Unfortunately, those days are long gone.

America's Founders understood the fallen nature of man. They knew what would happen if elected officials were allowed to pursue their self-interests without moral restraints. This is why they were determined to build our country on a foundation of biblical principles. They knew without a moral foundation, democratic politics would produce an amoral government in which right and wrong are determined not by scriptural truth but by majority vote—a government in which what is right is anything the ruling majority says it is. They also knew an amoral government would quickly become one in which those who govern serve themselves rather than the governed. As is now apparent, our Founders were prescient.

Lacking a moral compass, government becomes little more than a system for advancing the self-interests of elected officials in power at any given time and the government bureaucrats loyal to them. It matters little if these agendas are detrimental to the citizens government is supposed to serve. This is a hard truth you may have to share with fellow Americans who believe God has no place in government. The words of Psalm 33:12 will be especially relevant in these conversations: "Blessed is the nation whose God is the LORD, the people whom he has chosen as his heritage!"

When government serves elected officials rather than the citizens who elected them, the purpose of politics becomes nothing more than gaining and maintaining power. No longer is it about service to the country and its citizens. No longer are national interests put before personal interests. This is gutter politics, and it is where we are today in America. The more Americans are exposed to gutter politics, the less confident they become in their government. A lot of Americans believe, with good reason, that statesmanship and service to country have been replaced by self-interest and an obsession with power. A lot of Americans now believe "service" in Congress is just a way to feather one's own nest at the public's expense.

Americans at all points on the political spectrum are becoming fed up with the hyper-partisan bickering, character-assassination, and rank hypocrisy that characterize politics in the twenty-first century. They are growing weary of the politics of personal destruction and of gutter politicians who seek to destroy opponents rather than offering the American people better policies and better leadership. Disenchantment with gutter politics gives Christians an opportunity to reach out to their fellow Americans and show them a better way—the way of Christ. Statesmanship, service above self, and cooperation for the good of the country are possible, but not in an environment devoid of God and His Word.

FACTORS OF GUTTER POLITICS IN AMERICA

Several factors contribute to the transformation of America's political process into a gutter sport which have undermined the integrity of politics in America.

The first factor contributing to gutter politics is the growth of secularism. The number of professing Christians in America is declining. Whereas the church once influenced the culture, increasingly the culture influences the church. This has led to a general watering down of Christianity even among believers. In today's culture, too many churches seek the approval of the world rather than the approval of God.

Pastors focus exclusively on the love of God while steadfastly avoiding any discussion of God's hatred of sin and corresponding judgment. As the church's influence in American society has declined, constraints on public behavior have declined correspondingly. One of the inevitable effects of secularization is how it opens the door to the darker side of human nature, and the darker side of human nature shows through in gutter politics.

Another contributing factor is the rise of identity politics. People used to divide themselves into political camps based on issues, but that has changed. In today's increasingly godless culture, race, gender, age, sexual orientation, and other forms of group identity have become more important than issues. With identity politics, people come together in political alliances based on factors that divide rather than unite, factors such as race and sexual orientation. Identity politics encourages Americans to view the world from a tribal perspective which is the antithesis of the melting pot philosophy behind America's motto: *E Pluribus Unum.*

Another factor contributing to gutter politics is the rise of the '60s generation. In his inaugural address, President John F. Kennedy asked all Americans to focus on the things that unite us rather than the things that divide us. His request was ignored by the '60s generation, a generation rejecting traditional American and Christian values in favor of drugs, free love, and a feel-good, hedonistic approach to life. The youngsters of the '60s are now adults in positions of authority and influence as parents, grandparents, elected officials, college professors, doctors, teachers, lawyers, businesspeople, and even pastors. Many still retain their anti-America, anti-Christianity values from the '60s, and those values shape their political views.

Another contributing factor is the implosion of journalistic ethics. There were once standards, codes of ethics, and expectations of objectivity in journalism, but those days are long gone. Newspapers and television news programs have become openly partisan advocates for the political left or right, but mostly the left. This blatant polarization of the media has allowed gutter politicians to use the *court of public opinion* as a weapon for demeaning, defaming, and destroying political opponents.

The political left in America uses the mainstream media to carry out its principle borrowed from Hitler's henchman, Joseph Goebbels. As was explained earlier in this chapter, Goebbels believed if you told a lie often enough it would eventually be accepted as truth in the minds of listeners. Applying this principle has become standard practice among the Left. The death of truth in an era of gutter politics is just one more tragic consequence of rejecting God but accepting sin. To gutter politicians, truth is anything that serves their self-interested purposes.

A final factor contributing to gutter politics is the rise of social media. With social media, anyone anywhere can say anything about anybody and have it spread across the world in a matter of seconds. There is, however, an exception to this rule. Increasingly, Christians and conservatives are finding their postings on social media censored by the big-tech companies that own the platforms. Many Christians and conservatives are being de-platformed to deny them access to social media. Without access to social media, Christians and conservatives are limited in their ability to get their opinions and beliefs out to the public.

Social media postings at odds with the leftist views of the big tech companies controlling the platforms are regularly taken down and the posters expunged. By denying access to selected individuals in this way, social media firms are sending a clear message: agree with our views or lose your access to social media. Censoring and de-platforming Christians and conservatives is a favored strategy of the cancel culture.

The relative anonymity of the internet empowers users to engage in vicious, venomous attacks on people who hold views different from theirs. It also allows people to make unsubstantiated claims demonizing, discrediting, or marginalizing anyone they decide to target with their vitriol. These underhanded practices have contributed to the rise of gutter politics in America. It is important to understand the contributing factors presented herein, but it is even more important to understand they are not the root cause of gutter politics. The root cause runs much deeper.

ROOT CAUSE OF GUTTER POLITICS IN AMERICA

Politics descended into the gutter in this country because America is severing its Christian roots by rejecting God but accepting sin. All other factors related to this tragedy are ancillary to this root cause. The root cause of a problem is the one that, if removed, will eliminate the problem. If we stop rejecting God and reclaim the culture for Christ, politics will climb back up and out of the gutter. Return America to its Christian roots and then integrity, grace, collaboration, and mutual respect will be injected into politics. Continue to push God out of the political process and it will sink even deeper into the gutter.

When people wring their hands over the low state of politics in America and wonder what is happening to our country, it is tempting to ask, "Why are you surprised, and what did you expect?" Gutter politics is just one more of the tragic consequences inflicted on a nation rejecting God. America's Founders knew their grand experiment in self-government would be susceptible to the worst inclinations of human nature. This is why they sought to build our country on a strong moral foundation. We are now experiencing what the Founders feared. Because Americans are rejecting God, the political process is being guided by the worst inclinations of human nature.

The erosion of America's moral foundation has been a slow but steady process that began decades ago. Evidence of this gradual erosion can be seen in the declining number of people who self-identify as Christians in public opinion polls. For example, approximately 71 percent of Americans currently identify as Christians. On the surface, this appears to be an encouraging number, but when you consider it was 86 percent as recently as 1990 the picture changes, and not for the better.

To view the number of people who currently claim to be Christians from a more realistic perspective, consider that during the days of the Founders 99 percent of Americans identified as Christians. Add to this, claiming to be a Christian in an opinion poll does not make you one. Therefore, the real number is probably lower. Clearly our country is headed in the wrong direction when it comes to maintaining the moral foundation bequeathed to us by the Founders, a foundation based on Bible principles and Christian values.

The fastest growing faiths in America are Buddhism and Islam. Christianity, on the other hand, is declining. To complicate matters, Americans who profess Christianity no longer hold as strongly to the teachings of Scripture as did past generations. In many cases, churches water down biblical principles in an attempt to be acceptable to a broader audience. Rather than strive to be more acceptable to God, a lot of churches are focused on being more acceptable to society. I lament to say, the drift away from our Christian roots is occurring not just in contemporary culture, but in the church too. In many cases, society is influencing the church more than the church is influencing society.

HIGHER EDUCATION'S CONTRIBUTION TO GUTTER POLITICS

When it comes to assigning blame for the low state of politics in America, colleges and universities rank high on the list of complicit culprits. Few institutions have done more to drive politics into the gutter than the academy. This is because few institutions have contributed more to separating America from its Christian roots. It is ironic an anti-God environment would come to prevail in colleges and universities that began as Christian institutions.

The environment in higher education began to change rapidly and noticeably in the 1960s. Spurred on by the anti-war movement, the academy in America began to take a hard turn to the left, shedding its Christian heritage in the process. Since that time, colleges and universities have become ardent and persistent purveyors of secular-humanism. By turning generations of naïve, impressionable students away from God, colleges and universities have contributed substantially to the degradation of politics. In short, the political process in America resides in the gutter in part because colleges and universities have highly effective tools in the subversion of our national identity and heritage.

Colleges and universities preach tolerance while practicing intolerance. They profess inclusion while practicing exclusion. Their intolerance and exclusionary practices are aimed primarily at Christians and political conservatives. Rather than educate, institutions of higher education often indoctrinate. Academic freedom no longer protects those whose views are at odds with the dominant campus orthodoxy which, typically, is on the far left of the political spectrum. Marxist professors indoctrinate and manipulate morally and intellectually malleable students, transforming them into ardent acolytes of an anti-God worldview.

There have been monumental changes in higher education since the days of our Founders—disturbing changes. The earliest colleges and universities in America were all church-affiliated institutions. Harvard University, located in Cambridge, Massachusetts, is considered by many to be America's flagship university. Founded in 1636, the university is named after an early benefactor, John Harvard, a minister who bequeathed his library and half of his estate to the institution. Harvard's original mission—one far from its current mission—was to train ministers. Consider John Winthrop's description of Harvard's founding:

> After God had carried us safe to New England, and we had built our houses, provided necessaries for our livelihood, reared convenient places for God's worship, and led the civil government, one of the next things we longed for and looked after was to advance learning and perpetuate it to posterity. . . . And as we were thinking and consulting how to perfect this great work, it pleased God to stir up the heart of one Mr. Harvard (a godly gentlemen and lover of learning, there living among us) to give one-half of his estate . . . toward the founding of a college. . . . Over the college is Master Dunster . . . who has trained up his pupils in the tongues and arts, and so seasoned them with the principles of divinity and Christianity, that we to our great comfort (and in truth) beyond our hopes, beheld their progress in learning and godliness also.[1]

Many of Harvard's early graduates became ministers. Originally, the college's motto was *Veritas Christo et Ecclesiae*, which is Latin for "Truth in Christ and the Church." This motto has since been shortened to just one word: *Veritas*, which is Latin for truth. Unfortunately, Harvard no longer appears to accept Christ or the Bible as the source of truth, thus rendering its motto meaningless. The only source of truth is God's Word. Decision makers at Harvard would do well to heed the admonition in Proverbs 30:5: "Every word of God proves true; he is a shield to those who take refuge in him."

Harvard's rejection of God began long ago. One of the institution's earliest presidents, Increase Mather, grew disenchanted with what he viewed as the steady decline in the Christian views of Harvard's faculty and resigned as president. He was finished with Harvard but not with higher education.

Increase Mather and his son, Cotton Mather—a Puritan minister, historian, and prolific writer—helped establish a new college: the Collegiate School of Connecticut, now known as Yale University. Yale's other founders were Congregationalist ministers. Its founders were destined to be disappointed though. In spite of its Christian beginnings, Yale eventually followed in the footsteps of Harvard, transforming itself into a bastion of secular humanism.

In addition to Harvard and Yale, all of America's earliest and best-known universities including Princeton, Columbia, Brown, Rutgers, and Dartmouth were founded by Christians on Christian principles. Also like Harvard and Yale, these institutions have strayed far from their Christian roots. In fact, it would be difficult to find institutions in this country less friendly to Christianity than America's earliest and best-known universities.

There was a time when institutions of higher education in this country could be relied on to encourage the development of traditional Christian values in students. But those days are long gone. Now it is more common for colleges and universities to oppose Christian values and denigrate, demean, and defame anyone who holds them. When you consider the majority of America's elected officials and leaders in government are college graduates who were immersed for at least four years in leftist orthodoxy, it should come as no surprise that the political process now resides in the gutter.

A FINAL WORD ON GUTTER POLITICS

There are numerous studies available documenting such things as the decline in church attendance, the number of churches closing every year, and the percentage of young people who leave the church. However, you don't need to rely on dry statistical studies to find evidence of the tragic consequences our country is suffering by rejecting God but accepting sin. Just look around you.

Christians born in the 1950s and before can remember beginning each day in public school saying the Lord's Prayer, reading from the Bible, and reciting the Pledge of Allegiance. It was common practice for students who misbehaved to be required to copy passages out of the Bible or to memorize a Bible verse and recite it in front of the class. People of this generation who played high school football can remember a local pastor praying for both teams before every game.

Fast-forward to the present and try to imagine these things happening in a public school setting today. Since the early 1960s God has been unwelcome in our nation's public schools. Is it any wonder young people who spent their formative years in a godless environment where they were taught there are no absolute rights or wrongs would grow up to become practitioners of gutter politics? When the philosophy of life is *it's all about me*, it is no surprise the outcome is gutter politics.

Try to reconcile the politics of personal destruction and character assassination—the twin pillars of gutter politics—with the teachings of Scripture. Ephesians 4:32 admonishes us to be kind and compassionate to one another and to forgive each other just as Christ forgave us. First Peter 3:8 instructs us to love one another and to be compassionate and humble. Colossians 3:12 tells us to wrap ourselves in compassion, "kindness, humility, meekness, and patience." People who internalize these scriptural lessons do not engage in the politics of personal destruction, character assassination, or the other behaviors associated with gutter politics.

The farther our country drifts from its moral roots, the more often we are confronted by the dark side of human nature, not just in politics but in all aspects of our lives. The dark side of human nature directs the actions of gutter politicians who practice the politics of destruction. In turn, these practices threaten the future of the great experiment in republican self-government undertaken by our Founders more than 240 years ago.

In Mark 3:25, the Bible warns that a house divided against itself will fall. If the lack of a moral foundation causes the Founders' great experiment in self-government to fail, all Americans—including those who caused the failure by rejecting God—will suffer as a result. When the roof of a house collapses, it falls on everyone in the house. This is a truth you may want to share in love with practitioners of gutter politics. Their shady practices are going to cause the cultural roof in America to collapse and, when it does, they are going to suffer just as much as everyone else. When this happens, their well-worn tactic of pointing the finger of blame at others will not relieve them of their suffering.

In Matthew 28:18, Jesus says, "All authority in heaven and on earth has been given to me." Those who reject God but accept sin would do well to heed Christ's words in this passage from Scripture. God reigns supreme—not presidents, not members of Congress, not judges, and not governors. Gutter politicians may believe a numerical majority gives them the power to rule, but all authority resides with Christ—not a political party, no matter how large the party's majority may be. Politicians who ignore this fact eventually pay a price for their foolishness.

The truth is, Christ reigns supreme, a truth gutter politicians need to hear no matter how unwelcome it might be to them. People who gain power through practices such as the politics of personal destruction and character assassination eventually fall prey to their own perfidy. Further, even if they manage to escape the earthly consequences of their ways, there is still a day of judgment in their future.

WHAT YOU CAN DO ABOUT GUTTER POLITICS

To play a positive role in discouraging gutter politics, begin by studying what the Bible has to say about this reprehensible concept. To speak the truth about this issue, you must first know God's Word is the transcendent truth. Knowing what the Bible says about the politics of personal destruction and character assassination will equip you to speak the truth in love to people who engage in these sinful practices. Helpful verses for providing wise counsel to people who engage in gutter politics include the following:

- **Titus 3:9:** *"But avoid foolish controversies, genealogies, dissensions, and quarrels about the law, for they are unprofitable and worthless."* This verse may help show those who engage in gutter politics that cooperation and collaboration are the better way in the long run. It may also help you make the point that politicians in a pluralistic nation should learn to disagree without being disagreeable.

- **Psalm 33:12:** *"Blessed is the nation whose God is the LORD, the people whom he has chosen as his heritage!"* This verse may be helpful when you are trying to provide wise counsel to those who engage in gutter politics because they see themselves as little gods who should always have their way.

- **Matthew 28:18:** *"And Jesus came and said to them, 'All authority in heaven and on earth has been given to me.'"* This verse may help you provide wise counsel to gutter politicians and their followers who think having a voting majority on a given issue gives them authority. All authority resides in Christ regardless who has a voting majority at any point in time. Further, what is right and true is not determined by majority vote.

- **Philippians 3:20:** *"But our citizenship is in heaven, and from it we await a Savior, the Lord Jesus Christ."* This verse may help you provide comfort and reassurance to Christian brothers and sisters who are concerned about the direction politicians seem to be taking our country. As Christians, we should be good citizens and good stewards of the world God has given us, but we must never forget our citizenship on earth is temporary while our citizenship in heaven is eternal.

Once you have studied what Scripture teaches about gutter politics, pray God will change the hearts of those who engage in the politics of personal destruction and character assassination. Pray for those who engage in gutter politics as well as their victims. Also pray for people who are disturbed by the low state of politics in America. If you are not sure how to pray about this issue, recite the following prayer:

Lord, I am concerned about the state of politics in our country. Too many people are engaging in gutter politics; they are practicing the politics of personal destruction and character assassination. I pray You intercede on behalf of our country and turn us away from the current destructive path. Only by reclaiming the culture for Christ can we restore integrity, cooperation, and good faith to the political process in America. I pray You use me and my Christian brothers and sisters throughout our country as Your instruments in restoring Christ as the guiding light of American society. It is in the holy name of Jesus Christ I ask for Your intercession on behalf of America.

When you have prayed for our country, teach your own children and grandchildren the value of statesmanship, being able to disagree without being disagreeable, and service above self. Demonstrate by your example what these things mean on a practical level in everyday discourse. If we raise our children well, Christians can put a dent in gutter politics in just one generation.

Having studied the Bible, prayed, and taught your own children and grandchildren the value of statesmanship, service above self, and how to disagree without being disagreeable, try applying the following additional strategies:

- Set an example for your children, grandchildren, family members, friends, colleagues, and fellow church members of being able to disagree without being disagreeable.
- Refuse to support or vote for any politician at any level who engages in the politics of personal destruction or character assassination.
- Confront people who engage in the politics of personal destruction or character assassination or who are taken in by these practices. Use the information contained in this chapter to speak the truth in love to them about these practices and why you reject them.
- Encourage your church to take up the subject of gutter politics in Bible studies and prayer meetings so church members are well-informed about this issue and are not taken in by the politics of personal destruction or character assassination.
- Encourage your church's youth pastor to talk with young people who are coming of voting age about gutter politics, why it is wrong, and the role they can play in helping overcome it.

The politics of personal destruction and character assassination are less likely to occur in a Christ-centered culture. Be prepared to make this point when you speak the truth in love with unbelievers who are offended by these reprehensible practices as well as when you confront people who engage in them. When you talk with unbelievers who are put off by politicians who engage in gutter politics, let them know they cannot have it both ways. They cannot continue to reject God and expect there to be no consequences. Gutter politics is just one more example of what happens in a nation that rejects God but accepts sin.

CHAPTER 15

TEEN SUICIDE

Do you not know that you are God's temple and that
God's Spirit dwells in you? If anyone destroys God's temple,
God will destroy him. For God's temple is holy,
and you are that temple.

—1 Corinthians 3:16–17

Is there anything sadder than young people becoming so depressed they choose to take their own lives? Teenagers opting for this drastic and irreversible act at an age when they are just beginning life is one of the more tragic consequences associated with a culture devoid of Christ. Unfortunately, without God to lean on, many people, particularly teenagers, can become deeply depressed with their lives and look to suicide as an escape from the emotional pain.

Suicide is now the third leading cause of death for young people in America between the ages of fifteen and twenty-four. It is the second leading cause of death for people ten years of age and older.[1] Depression is closely associated with suicide. People who suffer from depression often turn to alcohol or drugs in search of relief. Predictably, this just makes the problem worse. When the bottle of alcohol or pills have been consumed and the effects pass, the depression is still there. The persistence of depression often leads young people to increase their use of alcohol and drugs, initiating a downward spiral that can lead to suicide, and often does.

Teenage girls are more likely than boys to attempt suicide, but boys are more likely to succeed in their attempts and die from suicide. In more than 50 percent of teenage suicides, guns are used.[2] As a Christian, it is important for you to understand teen suicide is not just an unnecessary tragedy; it is a preventable tragedy, one you can play an important role in helping prevent. What you can do is covered later in this chapter. But before getting into that, it is important for you to arm yourself with the facts about this tragedy.

FACTORS CONTRIBUTING TO TEEN SUICIDE

Depression is the most common cause of teen suicide, followed closely by mental illness. The two often overlap. However, there are several other factors related to teen suicide Christians should be aware of because these factors can lead to or magnify depression. Treating depression is not your job; it's not within the scope of what you can do to help prevent teen suicides. Depression should be treated by mental-health professionals, preferably ones using biblical understanding.

However, you might be able to help teenagers cope with some of the factors leading to depression if not confronted. Further, knowing the kinds of factors contributing to depression will help you know when it is wise to refer a teenager to mental-health professionals. Getting depressed teenagers into treatment before it is too late is one of the most important things you can do to help them. Recommending this kind of referral to a parent or guardian might just save the life of a troubled teenager.

The teenage years can be difficult, even for emotionally stable young people. Factors such as peer pressure, body changes, self-image, and the desire to fit in can weigh heavily on young people, particularly if they are not well-grounded emotionally. Add to these factors such common occurrences as parents divorcing, academic problems, the death of friends or loved ones, family relocations, sibling rivalries, a divorced parent remarrying, poor relationships with a stepparent or fellow stepchildren, being excluded from a school club, failing to make a school sports team, or conflict with a teacher or coach. All of these factors and many others not listed here can contribute to depression in teenagers. Worse yet, when social media is added to the mix the negativity associated with these factors is magnified.

RISK FACTORS AND WARNING SIGNS ASSOCIATED WITH TEEN SUICIDE

As was mentioned earlier but should be reiterated often, Christians—including ministers, youth pastors, and even biblical counselors—do not treat clinical depression in teenagers. That is the job of Christian mental-health professionals. However, there are two very important things individual Christians, ministers, youth pastors, and biblical counselors can do to help young people struggling with life.

The first thing Christians can do has already been mentioned in the preceding section: help young people cope with the predictable stressors teenagers often face. These stressors left unattended can lead to depression. Individual Christians, ministers, youth pastors, and biblical counselors can provide the support, reassurance, and guidance that may be missing in the lives of teenagers who are struggling with life in a fallen world. More importantly, they can point teens to Christ as the true and lasting source of support for coping with the problems troubling them.

The second thing Christians can do is watch for the warning signs and risk factors associated with teen suicide. When one or more of the risk factors are observed, the wise course of action is to observe the individuals in question closely and be prepared to get them into the hands of mental-health professionals on short notice. What follows are risk factors of which Christians who want to help reduce teen suicides should be aware:[3]

- Mental illness
- Family history of suicide
- Physical abuse (victim of)
- Sexual abuse (victim of)
- Losses (deaths of family members or friends, broken relationships, estrangement after relocating)
- Impulsive behavior
- Eating disorders (eating too much or too little)

- Financial problems
- Aggressive behavior
- Poor coping skills
- Unsupervised access to guns, knives, or other weapons that might be used to commit suicide
- Confusion over sexual orientation
- Feelings of being unloved or unwanted
- Personal insecurity
- Feelings of being misunderstood
- Divorce of parents
- Social rejection and loneliness
- Run-ins with law enforcement authorities
- Traumatic events (including events teens witness).

This list of risk factors has been validated by experience and substantial research, but it is not comprehensive. There can be other factors not listed here that put young people at risk of committing suicide. Further, to be clear, struggling with these factors doesn't necessarily mean a teenager is going to commit suicide. Rather, it means young people who are struggling with one or more of these risk factors bear watching; they are candidates for close observation by people who care about them. Those who do the observing should be prepared to put the individuals in question under the care of biblically-trained mental health professionals on short notice.

The most important resource Christians have in this struggle is prayer. It is Satan who wants these young people destroyed, and our prayer before the Throne of Grace is the most powerful weapon against the enemy.

It is important for anyone who wants to help reduce teen suicides to be aware of and sensitive to the known risk factors. It's as if you see a young person who cannot swim preparing to jump into the deep end of the pool. That individual may not drown, but he is certainly placing himself at risk of drowning. Because of the risk factor, appropriate action on your part is called for. Just as you would intervene to prevent this young man from drowning, you may need to intervene to prevent an *at-risk* teen from committing suicide.

In addition to the risk factors just listed, there are warning signs associated with teen suicide. Warning signs are a level above risk factors when it comes to how concerned you should be about the individual in question. Return to the example of the youngster who can't swim. Seeing him about to jump into the deep end of the pool would tell you he is at risk of drowning. Risk factors tell you to be observant in case action on your part is called for. If the youngster actually jumps into the pool and fails to surface, that would be a sign immediate action is called for.

Warning signs relating to suicide call for immediate action. Christians who want to play a positive role in reducing teen suicides should be familiar with the following warning signs:[4]

- Preoccupation with death in conversation, written assignments, artwork, and other forms of self-expression
- Intense, unrelenting sadness
- Feelings of hopelessness
- Lack of interest in activities, hobbies, or tasks that used to be important
- Withdrawal from family, friends, sports, social activities, school, or clubs
- Substance abuse (alcohol, drugs, or both)
- Unnatural sleep patterns (sleeping very little or sleeping all the time)
- Giving away possessions, especially valued possessions
- Lack of energy (especially in a usually energetic teen)
- Risky behaviors suggesting the teen doesn't care if he or she is injured or killed
- Inability to focus, think clearly, or concentrate
- Sudden absenteeism from school
- Sudden drop in performance in school
- Change in appetite (noticeable loss or increase)
- Increased irritability and bouts of anger.

The more of these warning signs a teenager exhibits, the more likely it is he or she will attempt suicide. What, then, is an appropriate response when you observe these types of warning signs in a teenager? Pray for insight and guidance. Don't ignore the signs and don't talk around the issue. Further, do not accept the misguided belief of some that anyone who talks about suicide is not going to go through with it. The rationale of these misguided individuals is if teens want to kill themselves they won't talk about it, they will do it. This belief is wrong. Young people often talk extensively about suicide before going through with it.

The best approach is to be forthright. Tell the teenager in question you have observed the signs and are worried he or she might be contemplating suicide. Be open with the young person, but non-judgmental. Make it clear you would like to help. No matter how teenagers react to your expression of concern, getting them professional help is always a good response when you observe one or more of the warning signs. This being the case, it is important for you to be familiar with sources of help available to struggling teenagers.

SOURCES OF HELP

This section profiles three organizations that can help, the kind of help they provide, and how to contact them. Christians who want to make a difference in reducing teen suicide should be sufficiently familiar with these organizations to know how to contact them and which to contact should the need arises.

CRU – Formerly Campus Crusade for Christ: https://www.cru.org/us/en/train-and-grow/life-and-relationships/hardships/suicide-prevention-resources.html

From the website: *No matter what you may be going through—the pain you may be feeling or the place you are at in your life—you are not alone. We want to help you or someone you may know who is facing depression or suicidal thoughts take steps toward health and healing. We have gathered some articles, resources and stories from others who have been where you are.* CRU is among the oldest and most respected international ministries. Applying biblical truth to real-world issues has been their key to success since 1951.

National Suicide Prevention Lifeline: 1-800-273-TALK (8255)

The National Suicide Prevention Lifeline is a network of local crisis centers covering the entire nation providing free and confidential support to people who are experiencing emotional distress or the warning signs of suicide. The Lifeline is open and available 24 hours a day, 7 days a week, 365 days a year. People who answer calls to the Lifeline are trained crisis counselors who know how to respond to emotionally distressed individuals and help them take a step back from the precipice and reconsider their suicidal thoughts. In addition to the telephone number given above, the Lifeline may be contacted online at www.suicidepreventionlifeline.org. This is the organization to contact for immediate assistance.

Stop a Suicide Today (stopasuicide.org)

Stop a Suicide Today is a school-based program that helps prevent suicides by teaching students how to recognize the warning signs and encouraging family members and friends to get at-risk teens in the care of mental-health professionals without delay. Key elements of Stop a Suicide Today's mission include connecting people as appropriate with crisis intervention counselors and/or emergency services, offering a free and anonymous interactive risk inventory on their website, reaching people who have attempted suicide or are contemplating it but have not received treatment, providing educational resources about all aspects of suicide, and maximizing utilization of the National Suicide Prevention Lifeline.[5]

WHAT YOU CAN DO ABOUT TEEN SUICIDE

To play a positive role in preventing teen suicides, begin by studying what the Bible has to say about this topic. Helpful verses for providing wise counsel to young people who exhibit the risk factors or warning signs of suicide include the following:

- **Psalm 34:17–18**: *"When the righteous cry for help, the LORD hears and delivers them out of all their troubles. The LORD is near the brokenhearted* *and saves the crushed in spirit.*" This verse may be helpful when you are trying to convince an individual you are concerned about to seek help or when you are recommending that individual's parents make a referral. The Lord is always present and available to walk them through their struggles.

- **Jeremiah 29:11**: *"For I know the plans I have for you, declares the LORD, plans for welfare and not for evil, to give you a future and a hope."* This verse may be useful when you are helping a struggling teen deal with the factors that can lead to depression. It may help a teen who feels hopeless realize there is hope in the Lord.

- **Proverbs 3:5–6**: *"Trust in the LORD with all your heart, and do not lean on your own understanding. In all your ways, acknowledge him, and he will make straight your paths."* This verse may be helpful when you are trying to point struggling teenagers to Christ rather than their peers for the comfort and acceptance they need. It can help you make the point the Lord is steadfast and dependable. Unlike the acceptance and approval of peers, God's love is unconditional.

- **1 Corinthians 6:20**: *"For you were bought with a price. So glorify God in your body."* This verse may be useful when you are trying to help struggling teenagers understand they have value no matter what their peers, siblings, or parents might tell them. If God loves them, they must be important. If Christ was willing to die on the cross for them, they certainly are important.

To speak the truth in love about suicide as part of the wise counsel you provide at-risk teens or their family members, you must first know the truth, and God's Word is the truth. Knowing what the Bible says about this issue will equip you to point the way to Christ for young people who may be contemplating suicide. The verses above are just to get you started. The Bible has much more to say about the issue of suicide.

Once you have studied what Scripture teaches about suicide, pray God will take hold of at-risk teens and fill the void in their hearts with the comfort, reassurance, acceptance, and resolve only Christ can provide. Pray for at-risk teens as well as family members and friends who are concerned about the warning signs they observe. If you are not sure how to pray about this issue, recite the following prayer:

Lord, I am concerned about (James). He is clearly at risk of committing suicide. I acknowledge only You can provide what is missing in this young person's life. Please wrap (James) in Your strong and loving arms and relieve him of the discouragement and depression that have him contemplating a tragic, irreversible act. Lord, will You also touch his family members and friends and help them know how to play a positive role in bringing (James) back from the precipice. I ask for Your intercession on behalf of (James) in this situation in the holy name of Jesus. Amen.

When you have prayed for the person you are concerned about as well as his family and friends, the next step is to make sure your children and grandchildren receive from you and the Lord those things missing in the lives of young people who are at risk of committing suicide. Give your children and grandchildren the time, attention, understanding, caring, and love they need from parents and grandparents. Encourage them to talk to you and listen attentively when they do. Help them learn to lean on you and on Christ for coping with the inevitable insecurities, disappointments, and discouragement that come with growing up in a fallen world. If we, as Christians, raise our children well, we can reduce teen suicide substantially in just one generation.

Having studied the Bible, prayed, and made sure your own children and grandchildren know a heart filled with Christ is the best way to cope with the inevitable struggles of life in a fallen world, here are some other things you can do to reduce this tragic consequence of living one's life without God:

- Memorize the factors putting young people at risk of developing a level of depression that can lead to suicide. When you observe any of these factors in the lives of teenagers, make an effort to help them cope in positive ways. Lead them to Christ and help them see how He is always there for them, even in their darkest moments. Your goal is to prevent the risk factors from pushing teenagers over the edge into depression.
- Memorize the warning signs relating to teen suicide. Be observant of and sensitive to these signs in teenagers you know. If you recognize a warning sign in a teenager, act immediately to get him or her

under the care of a mental-health professional. If the individual in question is not a family member, recommend his or her parents make an immediate referral.

- Make sure you know how to contact the National Suicide Prevention Lifeline and refer young people to this resource if you observe even one of the warning signs of teen suicide. If the young person in question is not a family member, recommend his or her parents make the connection. Familiarize yourself with Christian ministry resources like CRU.

- Discuss teen suicide with your pastor and recommend your church undertake the following activities: 1) Train your youth pastors on the factors putting young people at risk for suicide, how to recognize the warning signs, and how to contact the National Suicide Prevention Lifeline, 2) Train parents and grandparents of teens about the risk factors and warning signs relating to teen suicide as well as how to contact the National Suicide Prevention Lifeline (preferably this training would be open to the community as well as church's members), and 3) Train young people in the church and community based on the materials and resources available from CRU and Stop a Suicide.

There is less chance of teen suicides in a Christ-centered culture. Be prepared to speak this truth in love to family members and friends of teenagers who are struggling. When you talk with unbelievers who are concerned about teen suicide, help them see how Christ can fill the void in the hearts of young people who have been driven into depression by various risk factors. Help unbelievers see how rejecting God but accepting sin leads to tragedies such as teen suicide and this kind of tragedy is another example of what happens in a culture devoid of Christ. Let them know a step toward Christ is the first step away from teen suicide.

EPILOGUE

RECLAIMING THE CULTURE FOR CHRIST

For years, anti-God activists and organizations have worked relentlessly to remove all traces of Christ from the culture. They have used the courts, public schools, colleges and universities, the entertainment industry, and other culturally influential institutions as instruments in advancing their agenda to transform America into a godless society. Sadly, those who reject God but accept sin have made substantial progress toward achieving this goal, and the more progress they make the worse conditions become in America.

It's critical to remember who's behind this agenda. It's the same one who catalyzed the fall of mankind in the Garden. It's important we continue to engage him first and foremost as we wage war against Satan's compulsion with the destruction of God's creation. When we keep in mind who the real enemy is, we can do righteous battle against him while trying to rescue those under his power.

Without Christ at the center of our culture, we have become a nation where human life has little value, mob violence is common, mass shootings occur regularly, pornography is ubiquitous, the traditional family is imploding, abortion is celebrated, child abuse is epidemic, sexual slavery is a growth industry, politics is a gutter sport, drug and alcohol abuse kill more people than combat, and drivers shoot each other over minor inconveniences.

It is easy to sit back and point the finger of blame at anti-God advocates and organizations for darkening the culture, and they certainly deserve God's judgment if they remain unrepentant. However, there is a hard truth Christians must face. The anti-God crowd has succeeded to the extent it has because individual Christians and the church have not fought hard enough to keep Christ at the center of American culture.

Rather than obey Christ's command to occupy until He returns, too often we have shied away from conflict. Rather than rouse our churches to action, we have treated them as places of refuge for providing relief from the turbulence of a darkening culture. Instead of shining the light of Christ into the cultural darkness created by those who reject Him, we have sat back and let them have free rein to besmirch His name.

Too often Christians have wasted time and energy debating whether they should engage in the political process. While Christians have been bogged down in debate, Satan has taken advantage of their indecision. He has worked through his minions to use the political process against believers. Finally, as Christians, we have done too little to carry out the Great Commission: "Go therefore and make disciples of all the nations, baptizing them in the name of the Father and of the Son and of the Holy Spirit, teaching them to observe all that I have commanded you" (Matt. 28:19–20). Those we are supposed to reach out to and baptize include the secular adherents who reject God but accept sin.

All Americans are reaping what anti-God malcontents have sown. The cultural darkness resulting from their systematic rejection of God affects not just Christians but everyone, including them. Nothing can overcome the sad state of affairs in American society except the light of Christ, and it is our responsibility as Christians to be God's instruments in shining that light into the darkest corners of a godless culture. There is no other way to reclaim the culture for Christ. To do this, we will have to engage the enemy on six fronts: family, church, education, politics, law, and the public square.

- *Family.* The point has been stressed throughout this book that if we, as Christians, raise our children in biblical truth we can reclaim the culture for Christ in just one generation. Raising our children well means raising them in the discipline and admonition of the Lord. The strongest antidote against cultural darkness is a generation of men and women who accept Jesus Christ as their Lord and Savior and base all aspects of their lives on the teachings of Scripture. It is said charity begins at home. So does building a Christ-centered culture.

- **Church.** When Christians feel they are under attack, it is only natural to seek refuge among like-minded brothers and sisters in our churches. Our churches can be safe havens for recharging our batteries and gaining relief from the darkness of the culture. But our churches are not meant to be cocoons in which we wrap ourselves to avoid interacting with the world. The Great Commission requires more of us than this. Our churches must equip us to go out into the world wearing the armor of God so we can share His Word with unbelievers and carry out the Great Commission.

- **Education.** As Christians, we cannot justify turning the education of our children over to the anti-God propagandists who control the curriculums and content of our nation's public schools. Instead, we must commit to placing our children either in Christian schools, homeschooling them. It will do little good to take your children to church with you once or twice a week while placing them in an aggressively anti-God setting five days a week, particularly during their formative years. Christian children should not be left to fend for themselves in an environment hostile to everything their parents want them to believe and learn.

- **Courtroom.** Anti-God ideologues have long used lawsuits and threats of lawsuits to drive God out of our lives in America. Common sense suggests using the courts in this battle of worldviews should be a two-way street. It is time for Christians to turn this strategy around and go on the offensive. It is not enough for Christians to seek help from such outstanding organizations as Alliance Defending Freedom (ADF) only when they are attacked. The time has come for Christians to take the initiative and engage ADF and other supportive organizations in offensive actions. The best defense is a strong offense. Christians must make use of the courts to regain the religious freedoms taken from us by such organizations as the

Freedom From Religion Foundation (FFRF) and the American Civil Liberties Union (ACLU). It is time for individual Christians, churches, and Christian organizations to stop allowing anti-God organizations to treat them like punching bags that cannot fight back.

- *Politics.* While it is true God is in control, this fact should not be used as an excuse for ceding control of the political process to people who hate Him. God expects Christians to occupy until Christ returns for His bride and to be good stewards of what He has given us. Sitting back and allowing the anti-God crowd to control the political process is not good stewardship. The motto of Christians when it comes to politics should be *engage in the political process but don't depend on it.* Politicians will not reclaim the culture for Christ. On the other hand, they certainly have helped the anti-God crowd push Christ out of the culture. Engaging in politics means vocally opposing attacks on Christianity, writing letters to the editor of local newspapers, joining on-line discussions, participating in public meetings, encouraging Christians to seek public office, and supporting them when they do, and voting for the candidates whose views come closest to comporting with the Word of God. Don't expect political candidates to be perfect. Remember, you are not voting for your next pastor. You are voting for the men and women who will represent you in government. It should always be principle over personality in our voting decisions.

- *The Public Square.* Perhaps the most important contribution we can make as Christians in reclaiming the culture for Christ is to consistently reflect His image in every aspect of our lives. We can point unbelievers and fence-sitters to Christ by the example we set for them. By heeding Christ's admonition to love our neighbors as ourselves (Matt. 22:39), we can show atheists, agnostics, and the religiously ambivalent a better way. When they see Christ in action in our examples, even the most hardened anti-God crowd will find it difficult to deny His way is the better way.

If Christians will engage on all six of these fronts and persevere no matter how rocky the road back to a Christ-centered culture becomes, all Americans—including those who reject God—will benefit in the long run. Reclaiming the culture for Christ won't be easy, and it will take time. However, the challenges we face in reclaiming the culture pale in comparison to what we will face down the road if we shrink from this challenge.

ABOUT THE AUTHORS

Oliver L. North is a combat-decorated U.S. Marine, #1 best-selling author, founder of a small business, and holder of three U.S. patents. For seventeen years he was a syndicated columnist and host of *War Stories* on FOX News Channel. In May 2018, he retired from FOX News to serve as the 66th president of the National Rifle Association of America.

North was born in San Antonio, Texas, in 1943, graduated from the U.S. Naval Academy in 1968, and served twenty-two years as a U.S. Marine. His awards for service in combat include the Silver Star, the Bronze Star for valor, and two Purple Hearts for wounds in action.

From 1983–86 he served as Counter-Terrorism Coordinator on the National Security Council staff. He helped plan the rescue of U.S. students on Grenada, the liberation of American hostages, the capture of the *Achille Lauro* hijackers and the raids on Muammar Gadhafi's terror bases; after which he was targeted for assassination by Abu Nidal's Islamic Jihad. President Ronald Reagan described him as "an American hero."

North has authored nineteen best-selling books and is cofounder of Freedom Alliance, an organization serving wounded U.S. military personnel and their families. He is widely acclaimed for award-winning FOX News coverage of more than sixty U.S. units in combat and his Freedom Alliance "Hero College Scholarships" for children of service members killed or permanently disabled in the line of duty. He currently hosts a highly popular podcast on his YouTube channel, *Real American Heroes*. Yet, he says his greatest achievement is being "the God-fearing husband of one, father of four, and grandfather of eighteen."

LtCol North and his wife, Betsy, live in Virginia. In November 2018, they celebrated their 50th anniversary. He is currently founder and CEO of Fidelis Publishing and Fidelis Media.

Dr. David L. Goetsch is a Christian Counselor, a Presidential member of the American Association of Christian Counselors (AACC), church deacon, retired college professor, and author of more than seventy-five books. Several of his books are best-sellers that have been translated into various foreign languages. His books include *Christians on the Job—Winning at Work Without Compromising Your Faith* (Salem Books, an imprint of Regnery Publishing, 2019), *Christian Women on the Job—Excelling at Work Without Compromising Your Faith* (Fidelis Books, an imprint of Post Hill Press, 2020), and *Veterans' Lament: Is This the America Our Heroes Fought For?* (Fidelis Books, an imprint of Post Hill Press, 2020). Dr. Goetsch's weekly blog *Scripture in Action* may be accessed at www.david-goetsch.com.

NOTES

PREFACE

1. Robert Jeffress, Sermon titled "Cruise Ships or Battleships" aired on the Trinity Broadcast Network on January 24, 2021.

CHAPTER 2: TRAGIC CONSEQUENCES OF REJECTING GOD BUT ACCEPTING SIN

1. Mayflower Compact, accessed December 7, 2020, https://www.ushistory.org/documents/mayflower.htm.
2. Newt Gingrich, *Rediscovering God in America: Reflections on the Role of Faith in Our Nation's History and Future* (Nashville: Integrity House, 2006), 81.
3. Gingrich, 2.
4. Gingrich, 39.
5. Gingrich, 54.
6. Gingrich, 44.
7. Gingrich, 45.
8. David Barton, *American's Godly Heritage*, 3rd edition (Aledo, TX: Wallbuilders Press, 2017), 4–9.
9. Barton, 4–5.
10. Barton, 17.
11. Barton, 21.
12. Barton, 22.

CHAPTER 3: ABORTION

1. Cathy Cleaver Ruse and Rob Schwarzwalder, "The Best Pro-Life Arguments for Secular Audiences" (Family Research Council, Washington, D.C., 2020).
2. Robert M. Bowman Jr., "Argument for the Silent: A Biblical Case Against Abortion," April 1, 2001, https://reasons.org/explore/publications/facts-for-faith/read/facts-for-faith/2001/04/01/argument-for-the-silenta-biblical-case-against-abortion, pp. 1–2.
3. Bowman, 2.
4. Marjorie A. England, "What Is an Embryo?" *Life Before Birth* (London: Mosby-Wolfe, 1996).
5. Carl Sagan, *Billions and Billions* (New York: Random House, 1997), 163–79.
6. National Institutes of Health, MedlinePlus/Merriam-Webster Online, accessed December 18, 2020, www.merriam-webster.com/medlineplus/organism.
7. Ruse and Schwarzwalder, "The Best Pro-Life Arguments for Secular Audiences," 14.
8. Ruse and Schwarzwalder, 16.
9. Ruse and Schwarzwalder, 17.
10. Feminists for Life of America, accessed December 18, 2020, https://www.feministsforlife.org.
11. Focus on the Family, " Alternatives to Abortion: Pregnancy Resource Centers," accessed December 19, 2020, https://www.focusonthefamily.com/pro-life/alternatives-to-abortion-pregnancy-resource-centers/.

CHAPTER 4: GUN VIOLENCE AND MASS SHOOTINGS

1. "Gun Violence in America," updated April 27, 2021, https://everytownresearch.org/report/gun-violence-in-america/, pp. 1–7.
2. "This major Florida city has the most gun violence in the country, survey says," *Miami Herald*, November 19, 2019, miamiherald.com/news/state/florida/article237395479.html.
3. "Gun Violence in America," 6.
4. "Gun Violence in America," 7.
5. "Gun Violence in America," 7.

6. Smart, Rosanna and Scheli, Terry L. "Mass Shooting in the United States," Retrieved from https://www.rand,org/research/gun-policy/analysis/essays/mass-shootings,html on December 2, 2021.

CHAPTER 5: MOB VIOLENCE AND DEFUNDING THE POLICE

1. Brandon Christensen, "10 Deadliest Riots in U.S. History," June 1, 2020, https://www.realclearhistory.com/2020/06/01/10_deadliest_riots_in_us_history_494857.html.
2. Jemima McEvoy, "At Least 13 Cities Are Defunding Their Police Departments," August 13, 2020, https://www.forbes.com/sites/jemimamcevoy/2020/08/13/at-least-13-cities-are-defunding-their-police-departments/?sh=3e0dafa929e3.
3. Jeff Mordock, "Police counter protests, 'defund' push with retirements, resignations," *Washington Times*, August 13, 2020, https://washingtontimes.com/news/2020/aug/13/police-counter-protests-defund-push-retirements-re/.
4. Rachael Tillman, "Barr: Calls to Defund Police Contributed to Rise in Violent Crime," August 19, 2020, https://www.ny1.com/nyc/all-boroughs/news/2020/08/19/barr--calls-to-defund-police-contributed-to-rise-in-violent-crime.

CHAPTER 6: HUMAN TRAFFICKING

1. United States Department of State. "About Human Trafficking," Retrieved from https://www.state.gov/humantrafficking-about-human-trafficking/ on December 2, 2021.
2. Ibid.
3. Ibid.
4. Ibid.
5. National Center for Homeless Education. "Trafficking and the Commercial Exploitation of Children (CSEC)," Retrieved from nche,ed.gov/csec on December 2, 2021.
6. Christiane Sanderson, *The Seduction of Children: Empowering Parents and Teachers to Protect Children from Child Sexual Abuse* (London: Jessica Kingsley Publishers: 2004), 53.

7. National Human Trafficking Hotline, "Labor Trafficking," accessed December 29, 2020, https://humantraffickinghotline.org/type-trafficking/labor-trafficking.
8. "Labor Trafficking."
9. Andrew Kepler and Perry Chiaramonte, "Human trafficking victims depend on advocacy groups to bridge the gap to survival," Fox News, June 15, 2019, https://www.foxnews.com/us/human-trafficking-victims-depend-advocacy-groups-bridge-gap-to-survival.

CHAPTER 7: CHILD ABUSE AND NEGLECT

1. U.S. Administration for Children & Families, "Child Maltreatment 2019," updated June 3, 2021, https://www.acf.hhs.gov/cb/research-data-technology/statistics-research/child-maltreatment.
2. "Child Maltreatment 2019."
3. Child Welfare Information Gateway, "Definitions of Child Abuse & Neglect," accessed December 31, 2020, https://www.childwelfare.gov/topics/can/defining/.
4. "Definitions of Child Abuse & Neglect."
5. NOLO, "Emancipation of Minors," accessed December 31, 2020, nolo.com/legal-encyclopedia/emancipation-of-minors-32237.html on December 31, 2020.
6. Child Welfare Information Gateway, "Definitions of Child Abuse & Neglect."
7. U.S. Administration for Children & Families, "Child Maltreatment 2019."
8. "Child Maltreatment 2019."
9. Margherita Cameranesi et al., "Linking a History of Child Abuse to Adult Health Among Canadians: A Structural Equation Modeling Analysis," May 31, 2019, https://www.ncbi.nlm.nih.gov/pmc/articles/PMC6603908/.

CHAPTER 8: PORNOGRAPHY

1. Megan Hull, "Pornography Facts and Statistics," The Recovery Village, September, 29, 2021, therecoveryvillage.com/process-addiction/porn-addiction/related/pornography-statistics/.

2. "Ashcroft v. The Free Speech Coalition," 535 U.S. 234 (2002), accessed January 6, 2021, http://www.casebriefs.com/blog/law/constitutional-law/constitutional-law-keyed-to-cohen/restrictions-on-time-place-or-matter-of-expression/ashcroft-v-the-free-speech-coalition/.

3. Naughton, John. "The growth of internet porn tells us more about ourselves than technology," Retrieved from https://www.the guardian.com/commentisfree/2018/dec/30/internet-porn-says-more-about-ourselves-than-technology on December 3, 2021.

4. "Ashcroft v. The Free Speech Coalition."

5. U.S. Customs and Border Protection, "Importing into the United States: A Guide for Commercial Importers," last revised 2006, cbp.gov/sites/default/files/documents/Importing%20into%20the%20U.S.pdf.

6. THORN, "Technology has made it easier to harm kids," accessed January 7, 2021, https://www.thorn.org/child-sexual-exploitation-and-technology/.

7. The United States Department of Justice, "Citizens Guide to U.S. Federal Law on Child Pornography," accessed January 7, 2021, https://www.justice.gov/criminal-ceos/citizens-guide-us-federal-law-child-pornography.

8. "Citizens Guide to U.S. Federal Law on Child Pornography."

9. "Citizens Guide to U.S. Federal Law on Child Pornography."

10. Thorn, "Child Pornography," April 30, 2014, https://www.thorn.org/blog/redefining-child-pornography/. [This may be too old.]

11. Federal Bureau of Investigation, "What is Sextortion?," accessed January 7, 2021, https://www.fbi.gov/video-repository/newss-what-is-sextortion/view.

12. The United States Department of Justice, "Keeping Children Safe Online," updated October 25, 2021, https://www.justice.gov/coronavirus/keeping-children-safe-online.

CHAPTER 9: CANCEL CULTURE AND CENSORSHIP

1. National Archives, "America's Founding Documents," accessed January 8, 2021, archives.gov/founding-docs/bill-of-rights-transcript.

2. "America's Founding Documents."

CHAPTER 10: DRUG AND ALCOHOL ABUSE

1. American Addiction Centers, "Drug & Substance Abuse Statistics," Updated November 19, 2021, https://americanaddictioncenters.org/rehab-guide/addiction-statistics.
2. National Highway Traffic Safety Administration, "Drunk Driving," accessed January 15, 2021, https://www.nhtsa.gov/risky-driving/drunk-driving.
3. American Addiction Centers, "Drug & Substance Abuse Statistics."
4. "Drug & Substance Abuse Statistics."
5. IBISWorld, "Beer, Wine & Liquor Stores Industry in the U.S," Updated August 31, 2021, https://www.ibisworld.com/united-states/market-research-reports/beer-wine-liquor-stores-industry/.
6. "Beer, Wine & Liquor Stores Industry in the U.S."
7. National Highway Traffic Safety Administration, "Drunk Driving."
8. "Drunk Driving."
9. Journey Pure Emerald Coast, "22 Reasons Why People Use Drugs," accessed January 16, 2021, http://www.emeraldcoastjourneypure.com/top-reasons-people-use-drugs/.
10. Verywellmind. "How Drug Abuse Affects Our Society," Retrieved from https:www.verywellmind.com/what-are-the-costs-of-drug-abuse-to-society-63037 on December 3, 2021.
11. Addiction Center, "How Addiction Affects the Family," accessed January 19, 2021, https://www.addictioncenter.com/addiction/how-addiction-affects-the-family.
12. "How Addiction Affects the Family."

CHAPTER 11: CORRUPTION: LYING, CHEATING, AND STEALING

1. Eric Pianin, "Lying, cheating, stealing: How corrupt is America?" *The Week*, January 8, 2015, https://theweek.com/articles/467761/lying-cheating-stealing-how-corrupt-america.
2. Pianin, "Lying, cheating, stealing: How corrupt is America?"
3. Brandon Gaille, "25 Nose-Growing Statistics on Lying," May 20, 2017, https://brandongaille.com/25-nose-growing-statistics-on-lying/.

4. Hannah E. Meyers, "Thieves now mock the rule of law in 'progressive' cities like San Francisco," *New York Post*, June 17, 2021, https://nypost.com/2021/06/17/thieves-now-mock-the-rule-of-law-in-progressive-cities-like-san-francisco/.

5. Megan Leonhardt, "Consumers lost $56 billion to identity fraud last year—here's what to look out for," CNBC, March 23, 2021, https://www.cnbc.com/2021/03/23/consumers-lost-56-billion-dollars-to-identity-fraud-last-year.html.

6. Leonhardt, "Consumers lost $56 billion to identity fraud last year."

7. Chris Morris, "The number of data breaches in 2021 has already surpassed last year's total," *Fortune*, October 6, 2021, https://fortune.com/2021/10/06/data-breach-2021-2020-total-hacks/.

8. SafeHome, "10 Ways to Stop Criminals from Choosing Your Home," accessed January 15, 2021, https://www.safehome.org/blog/stop-criminals-from-choosing-your-home/.

9. Nationwide, "How to prevent car break-ins," accessed January 25, 2021, nationwide.com/lc/resources/auto-insurance/articles/smash-and-grab.

10. Consumer Reports, "10 steps on how to fight identity theft," January 17, 2015, accessed January 25, 2021, https://www.consumerreports.org/cro/news/2015/01/10-steps-to-fight-identity-theft/index.htm.

CHAPTER 12: ROAD RAGE AND SIDELINE RAGE

1. Taylor Covington, "Road Rage Statistics," Updated August 9, 2021, https://www.thezebra.com/resources/research/road-rage-statistics/.

2. Covington, "Road Rage Statistics."

3. Covington, "Road Rage Statistics."

4. Covington, "Road Rage Statistics."

5. Covington, "Road Rage Statistics."

6. "5 Crazy Cases of Road Rage," accessed January 26, 2021, https://www.idrivesafely.com/defensive-driving/trending/5-crazy-cases-road-rage.

7. "5 Crazy Cases of Road Rage."

8. Mueller, Walt. "The Age of Sideline Rage," The Center for Parent/Youth Understanding, Retrieved from https://cpyu.org/resource/the-age-of-sideline-rage/

CHAPTER 13: DEMISE OF THE TRADITIONAL FAMILY

1. Joint Economic Committee of Congress, "The Demise of the Happy Two-Parent Home," July 23, 2020, jec.senate.gov/public/index.cfm/republicans/2020/7/the-demise-of-the-happy-two-parent-home?fbclid=lwAR1Csk4L_ydljFo3UKpGLJVeF1CgpWe-fU6EPc27NUZAXMgnwxnl-hl4A.
2. "The Demise of the Happy Two-Parent Home."
3. "The Demise of the Happy Two-Parent Home."
4. Gillespie Shields, "Forty Facts about Two-Parent Families," accessed January 30, 2021, https://gillespieshields.com/40-facts-two-parent-families/.
5. Wilkinson & Finkbeiner, "Divorce Statistics and Facts," (2020), https://www.wf-lawyers.com/divorce-statistics-and-facts/.
6. "Divorce Statistics and Facts."
7. "Divorce Statistics and Facts."
8. "Divorce Statistics and Facts."

CHAPTER 14: GUTTER POLITICS

1. Albert Mohler Jr., "Harvard University's Founding Vision and Mission—A Timely Reminder," February 22, 2006, https://albertmohler.com/2006/02/22/harvard-universitys-founding-vision-and-mission-a-timely-reminder.

CHAPTER 15: TEEN SUICIDE

1. "Suicide Prevention: Youth Suicide," accessed February 9, 2021, https://web.archive.org/web/20170504155435/https://www.cdc.gov/ViolencePrevention/suicide/youth_suicide.html.
2. Boston Children's Hospital, "Suicide in Teens and Children Symptoms & Causes," accessed February 9, 2021, https://www.childrenshospital.org/conditions-and-treatments/conditions/s/suicide-and-teens.
3. "Suicide in Teens and Children Symptoms & Causes."
4. "Suicide in Teens and Children Symptoms & Causes."
5. Stop a Suicide Today, "Mission," accessed February 9, 2021, https://stopasuicide.org.